Titles in the Explore Ancient Civilizations Set

 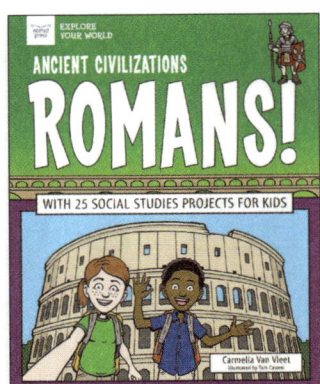  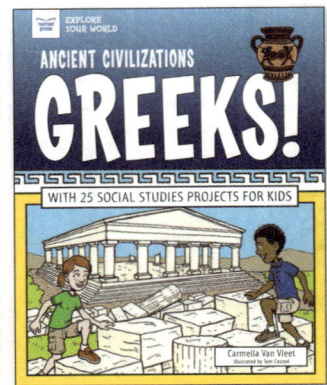

Check out more titles at www.nomadpress.net

Nomad Press

A division of Nomad Communications

10 9 8 7 6 5 4 3 2 1

Copyright © 2019 by Nomad Press. All rights reserved.

No part of this book may be reproduced in any form without permission in writing from the publisher, except by a reviewer who may quote brief passages in a review or **for limited educational use**. The trademark "Nomad Press" and the Nomad Press logo are trademarks of Nomad Communications, Inc.

This book was manufactured by Versa Press, East Peoria, Illinois
November 2019, Job # J19-07874
ISBN Softcover: 978-1-61930-842-8
ISBN Hardcover: 978-1-61930-839-8

Educational Consultant, Marla Conn

Questions regarding the ordering of this book should be addressed to
Nomad Press
2456 Christian St., White River Junction, VT 05001
www.nomadpress.net

Printed in the United States.

CONTENTS

Timeline . . . iv

Introduction . . . 1
Welcome to Ancient Greece!

Chapter 1 . . . 11
Welcome Home

Chapter 2 . . . 21
Let's Eat!

Chapter 3 . . . 32
Dress for Success

Chapter 4 . . . 40
School, Socrates, and Science

Chapter 5 . . . 51
The Olympics and Theater

Chapter 6 . . . 62
Democracy and War

Chapter 7 . . . 70
Gods, Goddesses, and Myths

Glossary ✷ Metric Conversions
Resources ✷ Essential Questions ✷ Index

 **Interested in primary sources? Look for this icon.** Use a smartphone or tablet app to scan the QR code and explore more! Photos are also primary sources because a photograph takes a picture at the moment something happens.

You can find a list of URLs on the Resources page. If the QR code doesn't work, try searching the internet with the Keyword Prompts to find other helpful sources.

→ 🔍 ANCIENT GREEKS

GREEKS!

C. 3000 BCE: People begin to settle in Athens, one of the most important cities in ancient Greece.

800 BCE: The height of the ancient Greek civilization begins.

776 BCE: The first Olympic Games take place.

C. NINTH OR EIGHTH CENTURY BCE: Homer creates the *Iliad* and the *Odyssey*.

600 BCE: The first Greek coins are made.

C. 569 BCE: Pythagoras, a famous Greek mathematician and scientist, is born.

C. 508 BCE: Democracy is born in Athens.

TIMELINE

146 BCE: Rome conquers much of Greece, making it part of the Roman Empire.

323 BCE: Alexander the Great dies and the ancient Greek civilization begins to decline.

86 BCE: The Romans tear down the Long Walls that helped protect ancient Athens.

332 BCE: Alexander the Great conquers Egypt and expands Greek civilization.

31 BCE: Roman troops conquer the last remaining Greek territories.

432 BCE: The Parthenon is completed.

447 BCE: Construction of the Parthenon begins in Athens.

468 BCE: Theater becomes popular in ancient Greece.

Many of the words and names in this book are hard to say, but you can hear them spoken online. Go to Merriam-Webster.com, search for the word, and press the 🔊 symbol next to your word to hear it spoken.

🔎 MERRIAM-WEBSTER

C. 470 BCE: Socrates, the famous Greek philosopher, is born.

INTRODUCTION
WELCOME TO ANCIENT GREECE!

Have you and your family or friends ever taken a group vote? Or looked up in the night sky at the constellation Orion? Maybe you've heard about the Trojan Horse, Achilles's heel, or the lost city of Atlantis. Guess what? All of these things came from ancient Greece.

Ancient Greece was an amazing civilization that reached its height of glory more than 2,000 years ago. You might wonder why we should care about people and things that existed thousands of years ago. But guess what? There are lots of reasons to learn about ancient histories!

WORDS TO KNOW

constellation: a group of stars in the sky that resembles a certain shape, such as the Big Dipper. There are 88 official constellations.

ancient: from an early time in history.

civilization: a community of people that is advanced in art, science, and government.

GREEKS!

economics: having to do with the resources and wealth of a country.

WORDS TO KNOW

First, learning about ancient civilizations helps us learn how we're all connected as humans. By studying communities that came before us, we can learn about how important things such as politics and religion and **economics** got started. We can also learn from the mistakes of the past. Finally, learning about ancient civilizations is fun!

What else can we thank the ancient Greeks for? Where was ancient Greece? And what was it like to live there? Let's find out!

DID YOU KNOW?

Have you ever heard the expression, "Those who don't learn from history are doomed to repeat it?" This is a way of saying that people can learn from events and avoid making some of the same mistakes of the past.

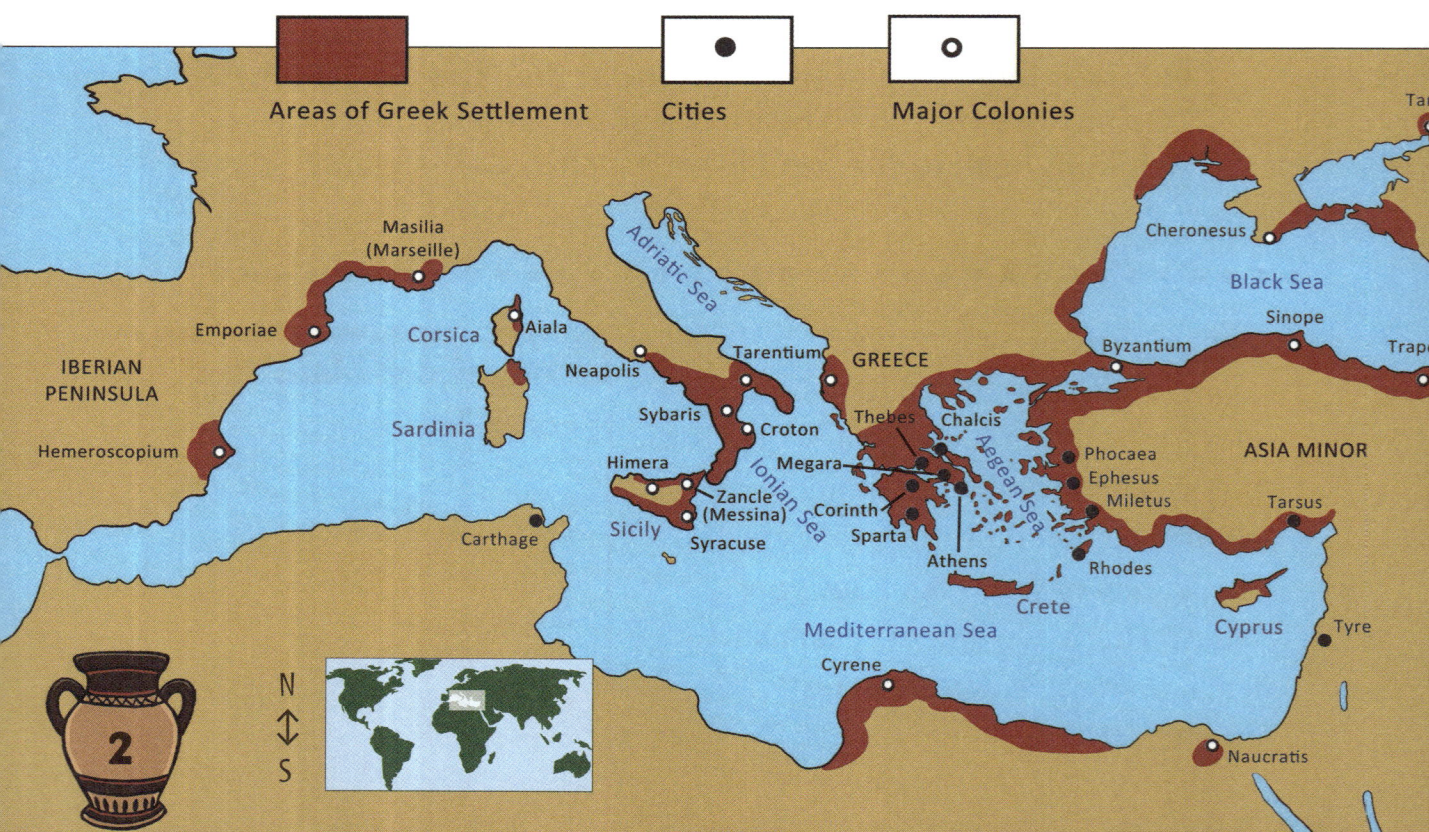

WELCOME TO ANCIENT GREECE!

WHERE IN THE WORLD

Today, Greece is a country in the southern part of Europe. The land of ancient Greece included modern-day Greece as well as hundreds of islands in the Aegean, Mediterranean, Adriatic, and Black Seas. Parts of modern-day Turkey, Italy, Egypt, and Spain were also part of the ancient Greek civilization.

Ancient Greece was at its height during the years between 800 and 31 BCE. It wasn't just one country or area. It was a collection of lands.

> **BCE:** put after a date, BCE stands for Before Common Era and counts down to zero. CE stands for Common Era and counts up from zero. These non-religious terms correspond to BC and AD. This book was printed in 2019 CE.
>
> **Hellenes:** the term used by ancient Greeks to describe themselves.
>
> **Hellas:** the term used by ancient Greeks to describe their region.
>
> **plains:** large, flat land areas.
>
> **WORDS TO KNOW**

You might be surprised to hear that the people of ancient Greece didn't call themselves Greek. They called themselves Hellenes. And they called their land Hellas. The words *Greece* and *Greeks* came from the ancient Roman people, who conquered the ancient Greeks beginning in 146 BCE.

The land of ancient Greece had lots of mountains. The coastline was jagged. Across large plains, farmers in ancient Greece grew crops and people settled in villages and towns. Winters could be very cold and snowy in the mountains, but most of the rest of ancient Greece was hot and dry, as Greece is today.

WHERE DID GREEK SHIPS GO WHEN THEY WERE SICK? TO THE DOC(K)!

GREEKS!

WORDS TO KNOW

city-state: an independent city that governs itself and the towns and land around it.

suburb: an area at the outer edges of a city, usually made up of homes with few businesses.

polis: a Greek city-state.

acropolis: a fortified high area or hill where people went during a battle.

Parthenon: a grand and famous temple in Athens dedicated to the goddess Athena.

temple: a building in which people worship gods and practice their religion.

trade: the buying, selling, or exchange of goods and services.

culture: the beliefs and way of life of a group of people.

CITY-STATES

Ancient Greece was made up of many *city-states*. A city-state was made up of a central city and surrounding towns and countryside. It's similar to how we have cities surrounded by *suburbs* today. The city-states were independent, meaning that each of them had its own government and ways of doing things. Each one even had its own kind of money.

The Greeks called a city-state a *polis*. People from the countryside and small towns went to the central city to buy things, visit friends, and conduct business. Each polis had an *acropolis*. An acropolis was a high area or hill that was fortified with walls. It was where people went if there was a battle. The acropolis gave the Greek people a safe place to gather and to watch for the enemy.

Athens was the biggest and most powerful city-state in ancient Greece. People began settling there around 3000 BCE. Athens was a bustling place with beautiful buildings and *temples*. Its rich farmland and big harbor made it a good place for *trading*. It was a place of great learning and *culture*.

DID YOU KNOW?

Athens's acropolis is one of the most famous in the world. It's where the Athenians built a famous temple called the *Parthenon*.

WELCOME TO ANCIENT GREECE!

> **democracy:** a form of government where the people participate.
>
> **military:** the armed forces of a country.
>
> **WORDS TO KNOW**

Some of the ancient world's greatest thinkers, scientists, and artists went to live in Athens. It was *the* place to be! And it was where **democracy**—government elected freely by the people—was born. Experts believe that around 500,000 people lived in and around Athens.

Sparta was another famous city-state. Like Athens, it was large and powerful and had plenty of good farmland. Early in its history, Sparta was bustling with art, music, and poetry. But when it was attacked by its neighbors, Sparta decided to build up its **military**.

Soon, Sparta had the strongest military force in ancient Greece. The Spartans had a reputation for being fierce warriors. To keep its army strong, the government of Sparta made every boy serve in the military. Boys left home when they were seven to begin training, which continued until age 30.

ATHENS AS IT LOOKS TODAY WITH ITS ACROPOLIS IN THE BACKGROUND

GREEKS!

> **WORDS TO KNOW**
>
> **astronomy:** the study of the sun, moon, stars, planets, and space.
>
> **Long Walls:** long stone walls that protected the road between Athens and its port of Piraeus.
>
> **parallel:** two lines always the same distance apart.

Boys were expected to learn how to run, fight, and jump and to be very fit. Even though they didn't serve in the military, Spartan girls also had to be fit. They had to train, too. People thought this helped them have healthy and strong babies. This was different from life for girls in Athens. Girls in Athens were kept indoors and didn't do much physical work.

For much of ancient Greek history, Sparta and Athens were enemies. There were times, though, when the two city-states fought together against a common enemy.

In this book, we'll learn more about ancient Greece, including the city of Athens, Mount Olympus, Helen of Troy, and the Spartans. You'll read about the birth of science, mathematics, astronomy, democracy, and even the Olympic games. Let's get started!

KEEP OUT!

Something that helped Athens survive and thrive were the **Long Walls**. These **parallel** stone walls, more than 65 feet high, protected the land between the city of Athens and the port of Piraeus. The walls were 525 feet apart and more than 20,000 feet long. During a war, they helped protect Athens from attack while keeping the route to the sea open. A route to the sea was important because that was how supplies arrived by ship. The Romans destroyed the Long Walls in 86 BCE. Do you think walls are a good way to protect a country? Are there other ways to defend an area?

WELCOME TO ANCIENT GREECE!

GOOD STUDY PRACTICES

Every good scholar keeps a study journal! Choose a notebook to use as your own study journal. Write down your ideas, observations, and comparisons as you read this book and do the projects. Some of the social studies projects focus on engineering while others are science experiments. Use the engineering design process or the scientific method worksheet to keep track of your observations and results.

Engineering Design Worksheet

Problem: What problem are we trying to solve?

Research: Has anything been invented to help solve the problem? What can we learn?

Question: Are there any special requirements for the device? What is it supposed to do?

Brainstorm: Draw lots of designs for your device and list the materials you are using!

Prototype: Build the design you drew during brainstorming. This is your prototype.

Results: Test your prototype and record your observations.

Evaluate: Analyze your test results. Do you need to make adjustments? Do you need to try a different prototype?

Scientific Method Worksheet

Question: What problem are we trying to solve?

Research: What information is already known?

Hypothesis/Prediction: What do I think the answer will be?

Equipment: What supplies do I need?

Method: What steps will I follow?

Results: What happened and why?

Evaluate: Analyze your test results. Do you need to make adjustments? Do you need to try a different prototype?

Each chapter of this book begins with an essential question to help guide your exploration of ancient Greece. Keep the question in your mind as you read the chapter. At the end of each chapter, use your study journal to record your thoughts and answers. Do your friends and classmates have different ideas?

> **? CONSIDER AND DISCUSS**
>
> How was ancient Greece similar to today's world?

PROJECT!

MAKE A FIELD NOTEBOOK

SUPPLIES
* recycled paper lunch bag
* scissors
* rubber cement
* 25–30 unruled notecards, 5 by 8 inches
* hole punch
* 2 one-inch book rings

Archaeologists are scientists who study ancient humans by looking at their **artifacts**. Archaeologists often keep track of their observations in field notebooks. You can make your own field notebook to help you record things you'd like to remember as you make your way through this book.

1 Crumple up your lunch bag. Next, carefully smooth it out on a flat surface. Don't worry if it has wrinkles—it's supposed to!

2 Cut the bottom off the bag and then cut along one side of the bag. Open the bag and lay it on a flat surface.

3 Spread rubber cement on one side of a notecard. Lay the notecard down on one side of the paper bag and press until the glue is dry. Spread rubber cement on another card and glue it to the other side of open paper bag.

4 Use the scissors to cut the cards out. Now you should have two covers that look like worn leather. Sandwich the rest of the notecards between the covers.

WORDS TO KNOW

archaeologist: a scientist who studies ancient people and their cultures through the objects they left behind.

artifact: an object made by people from past cultures, including tools, pottery, and jewelry.

antique: an object that's collectable or valuable because it is very old or historically important.

PROJECT!

5 Next, use the hole punch to punch two holes along the left side of the notecards. You probably won't be able to punch through all the cards at once. Try punching the holes a few cards at a time. Just make sure all the holes line up.

6 Insert a book ring through each hole. Now your field notebook is ready to use.

TRY THIS! Archaeologists have learned about ancient Greece by studying everyday objects, such as pottery. Ancient Greek pottery was decorated with lots of pictures. What can you learn about people just by studying pictures? Look at some old photographs. If you don't have any around your house, you can often find them at **antique** stores. Ask yourself: What can I tell about the people in the photos? What kinds of clothes are they wearing? What season is it? When was the photograph taken? What are the people doing? Are they having fun? Record your observations in your field notebook.

PROJECT!

PLAY "STORM THE ACROPOLIS"

SUPPLIES
* friends to play with
* hill (it doesn't have to be very high)

Ancient Greek city-states each had an acropolis on a high area or hill to help protect themselves. Here's a game you and your friends can play that shows the benefits of watching for an enemy from higher ground.

1 Choose one player to be the hoplite, which is a Greek foot solider. We'll learn more about hoplites in Chapter 6. This person should stand at the top of the hill, or "acropolis." All the other players remain at the bottom of the hill. If possible, the players should surround the hill so they'll be coming from all directions.

2 The hoplite closes his or her eyes. When they do, the other players try to sneak up the hill as fast as they can.

3 When the hoplite chooses, he or she yells "Stop!" and opens their eyes and looks around. The rest of the players must freeze in place. If the hoplite sees a player moving after they've yelled "Stop," that player must return to the bottom of the hill. Play continues until one person successfully reaches the top of the hill and tags the hoplite. That person then becomes the new hoplite, and the old one joins the rest of the players.

CONSIDER THIS! Does standing on higher ground make it easier or harder to see people approaching you?

CHAPTER 1
WELCOME HOME

Do you live in a house? An apartment? A mobile home? Do you live with other families or just yours? Lots of different kinds of homes are possible!

The homes of ancient Greeks were pretty plain and simple. Most of their houses were made from **mudbricks**. To make these bricks, ancient Greeks mixed mud, straw, and pebbles. Then, they poured the mixture into molds and let it dry in the sun.

Mudbricks were easy and cheap to make, but had problems. Mudbricks didn't last long and tended to crumble. Homeowners had to make frequent repairs.

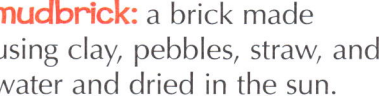

WORDS TO KNOW

mudbrick: a brick made using clay, pebbles, straw, and water and dried in the sun.

GREEKS!

WORDS TO KNOW

bust: a sculpture of a person's head, shoulders, and chest.

courtyard: the small open-roofed area in the center of an ancient Greek home.

exedra: a covered porch in ancient Greek homes.

ceramic: made from clay.

foundation: the base of a home that is partly underground and supports the weight of the building.

 INVESTIGATE

How were ancient Greek houses different on the outside and the inside?

The streets in Athens were narrow. Houses sat close together. They had one or two stories and no yards. Most had high, small, shuttered windows and were painted plain colors, such as white or tan.

The only decoration outside a house was a small stand with a **bust** of the god Hermes. Ancient Greeks believed Hermes kept evil from entering a house. Does your home have any good luck charms hanging outside?

STEP INSIDE

The insides of Greek houses centered around an open-roofed area called a **courtyard**. The sun shone into the courtyard, which often contained plants and fountains. Families liked to hang out around the courtyard and a nearby covered space called the **exedra**.

DID YOU KNOW?

Roofs were made from baked **ceramic** tiles, and **foundations** were made from stone.

WELCOME HOME

The main room of the house, called the **andron**, was used for entertaining. Greek men gathered here to eat and socialize. **Mosaics** often covered the floor of this room.

> **andron:** the area of a Greek home where the men entertained guests and held dinner parties.
>
> **mosaic:** a picture or design made from tiny tiles or stones set in cement.
>
> **WORDS TO KNOW**

Next to the andron was the kitchen, and near the kitchen was the bathroom. Inside the bathroom was a basin and a small, ceramic bathtub. Wealthy homes might even have a simple shower system.

The rest of the rooms surrounding the courtyard were bedrooms. Some houses had only one or two bedrooms. But rich people might have up to 10 bedrooms.

 Ancient Greek homes often had beautiful mosaic tile floors inside the andron. **Take a look at these examples, found in 2007 in southern Turkey.**

SCIENCE ALERT GREEK MOSAICS

GREEKS!

> **andronitis:** the men's area of an ancient Greek home.
>
> **slave:** a person who, in the eyes of the law, belongs to another person.
>
> **WORDS TO KNOW**

Ancient Greek homes had front doors to keep out intruders. But inside, rooms just had curtains to separate them from other areas of the house. Walls were decorated with pictures painted on wooden panels. Some had painted borders. At least one wall was often painted a bright color, such as dark red.

"NO GIRLS ALLOWED"

In ancient Greece, men and women spent their time in different parts of the home. The men's area was called the *andronitis*. Here, men met visitors, exercised, or just spent time together. Only grown men and male *slaves* were allowed in this part of the house.

ANCIENT GREEK MEN ATTEND A PROCESSION WITH THE GOD DIONYSUS

WELCOME HOME

The women's area of a home was called the **gynaeconitis**. All the female family members, female slaves, and boys under age six spent their time here. Wealthy ancient Greeks believed women should be protected from the outside world, so women of wealthier families usually stayed at home. They ran the household, took care of the children, and managed the money. They also spun wool and sewed all the clothes.

> **WORDS TO KNOW**
>
> **gynaeconitis:** the women's area of an ancient Greek home.
>
> **thalamos:** the master bedroom of an ancient Greek home.
>
> **oikos:** an ancient Greek household, including family members and slaves.

Poor women often worked alongside their husbands at shops and in the fields. Women did this in addition to their household work

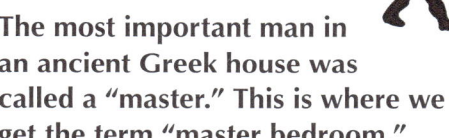

> **DID YOU KNOW?**
>
> The most important man in an ancient Greek house was called a "master." This is where we get the term "master bedroom."

Husbands and wives did share the largest bedroom, which Greeks called the **thalamos**. It was the room that had the most decorations and furniture.

OIKOS

Ancient Greeks didn't use the word "family." A household, including family members and slaves, was called the **oikos**. The male head of the oikos was completely in charge of everyone who lived in his house. Everyone had to obey him. There are communities in the world today that work this way, with a male at the head of the household. Is your family like this?

> **thronos:** a highly ornate, high-backed chair used in ancient Greece.
>
> **earthenware:** pottery made of fired clay.
>
> **brazier:** a small stove used in an ancient Greek home.
>
> **WORDS TO KNOW**

> **DID YOU KNOW?**
>
> Today, some Greek people wear evil eye charms or decorate their homes with them. These charms are the image of an eye set in a blue stone.

TAKE A SEAT

Ancient Greeks, both rich and poor, had few pieces of furniture. Tables were usually round, and some had three legs, others four. People sat on wooden chairs or stools. Furniture was often moved from room to room as needed.

The master of the house had a special chair called a thronos. It had arms and a high, padded seat. Sometimes, a thronos had carved legs that looked like animal feet. Couches and beds had wooden frames and leather webbing. Ancient Greeks used shelves, baskets, and earthenware vases for storage. Small stoves called braziers heated their houses. And oil lamps gave light!

What was life like in these cozy homes? We'll take a look in the next chapter!

WHAT DID THE ANCIENT GREEK CHILD CALL HIS THREE-LEGGED CHAIR?

A cool stool!

 CONSIDER AND DISCUSS

It's time to consider and discuss: How were ancient Greek houses different on the outside and the inside?

PROJECT!

MAKE A MODEL OF AN OIL LAMP

SUPPLIES
* wax paper
* air-hardening clay
* toothpick
* craft paint
* battery-operated votive candle

Ancient Greek oil lamps were made from terra-cotta, bronze, or silver, so look for those paint colors for this project.

1 Cover your work area with wax paper. Mold most of your clay into a shallow bowl about 6 inches in diameter. This is the base of your lamp.

2 Roll a medium-sized piece of clay into a log 5 inches long and about as thick as your finger. Gently curve the log into a "C" shape for the lamp's handle. Attach the handle to the lamp.

3 Use the toothpick to carve designs or a picture into the outside of the lamp. Let the clay dry. When the lamp is hard, paint it.

4 Add your battery-operated votive candle and your lamp is ready to use!

THINK ABOUT IT! Ancient Greeks primarily used olive oil to fuel their lamps. Today, we use different types of fuel, or energy, for our lights, running our cars, or operating appliances. Which fuels help our environment? Which ones hurt it?

WORDS TO KNOW

terra-cotta: earthen clay used as a building material, for pottery, and for sculptures.

diameter: the line through the center of a circle, from one side to the other.

PROJECT!

MAKE A COURTYARD COLUMN

Ancient Greeks are known for the marble columns in their buildings. In this project you will make a plain Doric column.

> **SUPPLIES**
> * newspaper
> * empty toilet paper roll
> * cardboard
> * pencil
> * scissors
> * paint brush
> * paint—gold, black, white
> * paper towel
> * toothpick
> * glue

1 Cover your workspace with newspaper. Stand the toilet paper roll on top of the cardboard. Carefully draw two matching circles that are slightly bigger than the end of the roll. Cut the circles out with the scissors.

2 Paint the tops and bottoms of the cardboard circles gold. Set them aside. Paint the outside of the toilet paper roll black. Let it dry for a few minutes.

3 Crumple up the paper towel and dip it into a small bit of white paint. Dab the white paint all over the black paint to create a marbled effect. Let the white paint dry for a few minutes.

4 Dip the end of the toothpick in white paint. Drag the toothpick along the column to make skinny parallel lines at an angle. Don't worry if they aren't the same. It looks more realistic if they aren't. These lines are the marble's veins.

> **WORDS TO KNOW**
>
> **column:** a tall, thick post that holds up part of a building.
>
> **Doric column:** a Greek column with a plain top.

18

PROJECT!

EXAMPLES OF MARBLE

5 Dab a corner of the paper towel (or your finger) along the white veins to lightly blend the paint. Let the paint dry.

6 When the paint is dry, glue the gold pieces to the top and bottom of the column.

THINK ABOUT IT! Marble is a type of rock formed when limestone (another type of rock) is under a great deal pressure for a very long time. What color is marble usually? What other colors can it be? What gives marble its color? Do some research!

PROJECT!

MAKE A MOSAIC

You can create a painting that looks like a Greek mosaic made with round stones.

SUPPLIES
* foam board (cut to any size you'd like)
* pencil
* 2 dozen Q-tips
* acrylic paint in various colors
* newspaper

1 Cover your workspace with newspaper. Lay the foam board on top.

2 Lightly sketch a picture on your foam board. Some mosaics were of people. Others were of objects, landscapes, or patterned designs.

> **DID YOU KNOW?**
> Greek homes had no toilets. People used **chamber pots** that were emptied into the streets.

3 When you're happy with your sketch, you can begin painting. Dip the end of a Q-tip in paint and then press it on the foam board to make a dot. Use dots to go over the outline and fill in your sketch. Be patient. This might take a long time! Use a different Q-tip for each color of paint.

4 Greek homes often had floors covered with mosaics. But when the paint is dry, you can hang your mosaic up on the wall.

> **TRY THIS!** Instead of dots of paint, create a mosaic using broken tile pieces, small, glass stones (available at craft stores), coins, bottlecaps, or other items.

WORDS TO KNOW

chamber pot: a large, bowl-shaped pot used as an indoor toilet.

CHAPTER 2
LET'S EAT!

What did you have for breakfast this morning? Are you a vegetarian or do you eat meat? Many of the food choices we make today are ones the ancient Greeks faced in the past. Some of the foods we eat are the same, too!

For ancient Greeks, breakfast was usually simple, often a piece of bread and some wine. Lunch may have been just bread and a piece of cheese or fruit. Dinner was the main meal of the day and included bread, cheese, fruits, vegetables, and wine.

> **? INVESTIGATE**
>
> What crops were important to ancient Greeks?

21

GREEKS!

Words to Know

vegetarian: someone who doesn't eat meat.

garos: a sauce made from old fish, used in ancient Greece.

agora: the open marketplace in the middle of an ancient Greek town.

kline: a long couch on which guests lay at ancient Greek dinner parties.

philosophy: the study of truth, wisdom, the nature of reality, and knowledge.

Women cooked on grills over open fires or in small clay ovens. Ancient Greeks used spices, including cinnamon and cloves, and sweeteners, such as honey, when cooking. They also used a bad-smelling sauce made from old fish, called **garos**, to flavor foods.

FARM LIFE

Many of the people who lived around Athens were farmers. The valleys and the land along the coastlines had rich soil where farmers grew all kinds of crops. These included grapes, figs, lettuce, garlic, carrots, leeks, cucumbers, artichokes, beets, lentils, peas, onions, and cabbage. Any food the farmers and their families didn't eat themselves was sold at the market in the town square, called the **agora**.

PARTY TIME!

Wealthy ancient Greeks liked to throw fancy dinner parties. These parties were for men only. Guests would lie on long couches called **klines** with small tables in front of them. They ate a variety of breads, cheeses, vegetables, and fish. For dessert, partygoers dined on fruit, cakes, and a sweet dish called baklava made with layers of pastry and honey. Musicians, dancers, and acrobats entertained guests. Afterward, guests discussed serious topics such as politics and **philosophy**, recited poetry, or sang hymns.

LET'S EAT!

THE TEMPLE OF HEPHAESTUS, WHICH STOOD IN THE ATHENS AGORA

Wheat and barley were important crops, too. Ancient Greeks used them to make bread and a watery porridge. Bread was served at all meals. People used it to soak up sauces and scoop up food.

OLIVE, GRAPES, AND MEAT

Olives and grapes were the most important crops in ancient Greece. People ate olives, and pressed them for their oil to be used in cooking, as fuel for lamps, as soap, and in makeup and medicine.

DID YOU KNOW?

In addition to bathing in small bathtubs, ancient Greeks cleaned themselves by rubbing oil on their skin, then scraping the oil (and the dirt) off.

GREEKS!

> **Dionysus:** the god of wine.
>
> **ferment:** when a substance breaks down over time into another substance, such as grape juice turning into wine.
>
> **amphorae:** pottery jars used to store wine and olive oil.
>
> **WORDS TO KNOW**

Grapes were for wine, which was a big part of daily life. Every year, the ancient Greeks held celebrations in honor of **Dionysus**, the god of wine.

When the grapes were ready in the fall, the ancient Greeks put them into big tubs. Workers stomped on the grapes with their bare feet! Then, the juice was left to **ferment** in goatskin containers. Finally, the wine was stored in rounded, clay containers with skinny necks called **amphorae**.

DID YOU KNOW?

Ancient Greeks didn't use forks or spoons. They ate with their fingers.

LET'S EAT!

LIFE ON A VASE

Ancient Greeks are famous for their beautiful pottery. Greek pottery is usually known as "black figure" or "red figure." Black-figure pottery had red backgrounds with black figures. Red-figure pottery had black backgrounds with red figures.

 Much of what we know about ancient Greek life was learned by studying these vases.

🔍 THORVALDSEN H526

Farmers kept oxen to help plow the soil. They also had sheep, goats, and poultry. Most animals were kept for milk or eggs.

Many ancient Greeks shared similar diets, though the rich enjoyed some foods that the poor could not—for example, they ate meat more often. Poor ancient Greeks didn't eat very much meat. In fact, the only time many ancient Greeks ate meat was when an animal was killed to honor a god. Most Greeks ate lots of fish, though.

What did most Greeks wear? Let's find out!

KNOCK, KNOCK. WHO'S THERE? OLIVE. OLIVE WHO? Olive it when you get my jokes!

 CONSIDER AND DISCUSS

It's time to consider and discuss: What crops were important to ancient Greeks?

PROJECT!

MAKE A KYLIX

A **kylix** is a two-handled cup the ancient Greeks used. When they weren't drinking from it, the family hung the cup on the wall, by one of the handles, for decoration.

SUPPLIES
* newspaper
* clean and dry 8-ounce plastic container with lid
* scissors
* masking tape
* empty paper towel roll
* plaster cloth (sometimes called plaster gauze, found at craft stores)
* shallow bowl of water
* paintbrush
* reddish-brown paint
* black paint

1 Spread the newspaper over your workspace. Set the lid of the plastic container to one side for now. Carefully cut the container in half so the bottom half makes a shallow cup.

2 From the top piece of plastic that's left, cut two pieces that are 6 inches long and about three-quarters of an inch wide.

3 Bend the pieces of plastic to create handles. Use the masking tape to attach the handles to each side of the shallow cup.

4 Cut the paper towel roll in half. Tape one end to the bottom of the cup. This is the "stem" of your cup.

5 Tape the other end of the stem onto the lid of the container. The lid is the base of your kylix.

WORDS TO KNOW

kylix: a shallow, two-handled cup used for drinking wine.

PROJECT!

6 Cut the plaster cloth into small pieces, each about the size of a playing card. One at a time, dip the pieces of plaster cloth into the water and begin placing them on the cup. Cover the whole cup (including the handles, stem, and base) in several layers of plaster cloth. Smooth out any bumps with your wet fingers.

7 Let the cup dry completely. Then, paint it with a coat of the reddish-brown paint.

8 Once the paint is dry, paint a scene or add designs using the black paint. Don't drink out of your kylix, but have fun pretending! Hang your cup up for display.

A KYLIX FROM ANCIENT GREECE

THINK ABOUT IT! Does your family display any items when you're not using them? What is beautiful about them?

PROJECT!

MAKE OLIVE OIL SOAP

Ancient Greeks used olive oil for many things, including soap! Give it a try.

Note: Ask an adult to help with the microwave and with the grater.

SUPPLIES
* 1–2 bars white, unscented soap
* cheese grater
* microwave-safe bowl
* ¼ cup water
* 3 tablespoons olive oil
* wooden spoon
* essential oil, such as lavender oil (optional)
* soap molds (found at craft stores)

1 Use the cheese grater to grate the soap into the bowl. Be careful not to scrape your fingers. You will need 1½ cups of grated soap.

2 Pour the water on top of the soap shavings, but don't mix it in.

3 Put the soap in the microwave for 30 seconds to melt. Check to see if the soap is melted. If it's not, return it to the microwave for another 30 seconds. Keep doing this for 30 seconds at a time until the soap is liquid.

4 Add the olive oil and use the spoon to mix the soap and oil together. If you want, can add 5 to 10 drops of essential oil to give the soap a scent.

PROJECT!

WINE COUNTRY

Everyone drank wine in ancient Greece and it was served with most meals. Winemakers put water in the wine, though, and the water diluted the syrupy wine. Ancient Greek wine was about one-part wine and two-parts water. It was considered **uncivilized** to drink wine that wasn't watered down. It was also highly unacceptable to be drunk in public. As with olives and olive oil, ancient Greeks sold wine to nearby countries.

5 Carefully pour your soap into the molds and let it set until it **solidifies**. Depending on how big your molds are, this might take a day. Once the soap is completely cooled, remove it from the molds and use it.

TRY THIS! Solid materials such as soap have a **melting point**. The melting point of soap is approximately 125 degrees Fahrenheit (51 degrees Celsius). Which of these materials do you think has the lowest melting point? Why do you think this? Can you think of a way to test your hypothesis?

1. Paraffin wax
2. Butter
3. Ice cream

WORDS TO KNOW

uncivilized: crude, not very advanced.

solidify: to become hard or solid.

melting point: the temperature at which a solid becomes a liquid.

PROJECT!

HOST A SYMPOSIUM

SUPPLIES
* pillows
* cups and plates
* snack food you can eat with you fingers
* grape juice
* lots of friends

A **symposium** was a party where Greek men gathered to eat, drink, and discuss topics. Hosting your own symposium is easy and fun!

1 Invite your friends over. Ancient Greek symposiums were strictly for men, but you can include boys and girls.

2 Lay some pillows on the floor to create your own version of a kline for each guest. Place plates of bite-size food in front of your guests. For example, offer grapes and other fruits, bread, and vegetables. You could even make a Greek salad! Give everyone a cup of grape juice to drink.

TRY THIS! Greek symposiums often included partygoers playing instruments. Make your own instruments to add to your symposium.

3 Listen to music, tell jokes or stories, and discuss important (or funny) topics while you eat.

DID YOU KNOW?

To keep their drinks cold, ancient Greeks put them in special vessels underground where it was cooler. Rich people might have someone haul ice down from the mountains, but with no freezers, people had to fetch new ice every day!

WORDS TO KNOW

symposium: a party where Greek men gathered to eat, drink, and discuss topics.

PROJECT!

BLACK-FIGURE VASE

We know a lot about ancient Greece by studying their vases, which illustrated everyday life. Want to tell future archaeologists about your life? Make your own Greek-style vase.

SUPPLIES
* terra-cotta pot or vase, any size
* pencil
* black, acrylic paint
* thin paint brush
* newspaper
* spray shellac (available at craft stores)

1 Brainstorm a scene or story from your life that you could sketch. For example, playing a sport, reading, cooking, or visiting an amusement park. Use your pencil to sketch this scene around your terra-cotta pot. Keep in mind that ancient Greek black-figured and red-figured pottery usually showed figures in profile, from the side.

2 When your sketch is ready, spread newspaper around your workspace. Place your pot on top of the newspaper and begin painting. Let your pottery dry.

3 When your paint is dry, spray the outside of the pot with shellac. Make sure to spray paint in a well-vented area and to protect your work area with newspaper.

CONSIDER THIS! The artists who painted ancient Greek vases typically worked together in a shop under the direction of a master potter. Can you think of some reasons why working together in a group like this might be a benefit?

CHAPTER 3
DRESS FOR SUCCESS

What are you wearing today? Shorts, jeans, T-shirt? Maybe you're more dressed up than that. Most ancient Greeks took a lot of pride in how they looked. They believed people should look their best at all times. Even though clothes in ancient Greece were fairly simple, they were still quite beautiful.

Clothes were also practical! Much of Greece is sunny and hot, so most clothes were made of lightweight fabric that helped keep people cool. Sometimes, the cloth was so lightweight that you could see through it. The ancient Greeks weren't shy about their bodies!

INVESTIGATE

How does the climate affect what you wear?

DRESS FOR SUCCESS

BASIC OUTFITS

> **WORDS TO KNOW**
>
> **chiton:** a basic piece of clothing that men and women wore in ancient Greek times.

In ancient Greece, men and women wore the same piece of clothing, called a **chiton**. A chiton was made from a rectangular piece of material cut into two pieces, which were then fastened at intervals across the shoulders and arms. You put on a chiton by pulling it over your head, just like a T-shirt, and then wrapping a belt around your waist. Chitons looked like loose, sleeveless dresses.

Women wore chitons that fell to their ankles. Men usually wore chitons that went to their knees.

> **DID YOU KNOW?**
>
> People sold clothes at the agora. But most ancient Greeks made their own clothes at home.

Men sometimes wore longer chitons for parties or formal business.

Children also wore knee-length chitons. They needed clothes that let them run around and move easily.

A STATUE OF A WOMAN DRESSED IN A CHITON
CREDIT: ELGIN COLLECTION, BRITISH MUSEUM

GREEKS!

> **accessory:** something, often jewelry, added to make an outfit more attractive.
>
> **brooch:** a special pin.
>
> **himation:** a large piece of material that the ancient Greeks wore over their shoulders.
>
> **chlamys:** a short cloak worn by ancient Greeks.
>
> **climate:** the long-term weather patterns of a particular area of land.
>
> **petasos:** a flat, wide-brimmed hat that ancient Greeks wore.
>
> **veil:** a thin covering that goes over a person's head.
>
> **WORDS TO KNOW**

Though everyone wore the same basic clothing, the accessories and fabric colors were different. Some ancient Greeks fastened their chitons with simple buttons. Others used fancy brooches or pins made of ivory or gold. If you were poor, your chiton was white. Wealthy people could afford to have their clothes dyed bright shades of red or purple.

Sometimes, people wore belts to jazz up their outfits! Himations also added color and warmth. A himation was a large rectangular piece of material. Women draped them around their shoulders like shawls. Men often just draped them over one shoulder.

A chlamys was a shorter version of a himation. They were the ancient Greek version of a jacket.

KEEPING COOL

The climate in ancient Greece was sunny and hot! It was important for people to protect themselves from the sun. Ancient Greek men wore a round, felt hat called a petasos. It had a wide brim to keep the sun off the wearer's face. When women went out, they often wore veils to protect their heads and faces from the sun.

> **DID YOU KNOW?**
>
> Though ancient Greek women typically wore long chitons, they wore short ones for work.

DRESS FOR SUCCESS

Ancient Greeks thought suntans were unattractive. Pale skin meant you were wealthy enough that you didn't have to work outdoors. Some women used powder to make their skin look paler.

 We know how the ancient Greeks dressed by looking at the art on pottery and by studying statues from that time. **Take a look!**

🔍 MET ANCIENT GREEK DRESS

Men kept their hair short and didn't usually grow beards or mustaches. Long hair was the fashion for women, but it was often pulled up or braided—which was a lot cooler. Women used headbands, nets, ribbons, and hairpins to keep their hair in place.

TWO WOMEN HOLD FLOWERS, C. 470 BCE. SEE HOW THEIR HAIRSTYLES ARE PULLED UP AND BACK?
EXCAVATED BY LÉON HEUZEY AND HENRI DAUMET; PLACE: PHARSALOS IN THE REGION OF THESSALY

GREEKS!

SHOE SURVEY

Ancient Greeks tried to avoid wearing shoes whenever they could, especially at home. How many people today choose not to wear shoes while at home? Ask a variety of people, such as family, friends, neighbors, and people in your community, if they wear shoes at home. Keep track of their ages and responses in your field notebook. Next, create a graph showing how many people wear shoes and how many people go barefoot at home. Does the age of the person seem to affect their response? Do some communities show a stronger response one way or the other? Do some research into the practice of wearing shoes at home in other countries. What do you find out?

DID YOU KNOW?

Ancient Greek women wore lots of jewelry—rings, brooches, bracelets, necklaces, and earrings were popular. These items were usually big and fancy and were often made of gold and silver.

What about their feet? When they were indoors, ancient Greeks went barefoot. But outside, they wore leather sandals to protect their feet from the hot ground. These sandals had laces that wrapped around a person's ankles or legs. Workers and soldiers wore leather boots.

And where did people go wearing their cool clothing? If you were a kid, you might go to school! We'll learn more about daily life in the next chapter.

CONSIDER AND DISCUSS

It's time to consider and discuss: How does the climate affect what you wear?

PROJECT!

MAKE A CHITON

Chitons were a popular piece of clothing worn in ancient Greece by both men and women. You can make your own!

SUPPLIES
* 2 rectangular pieces of linen or cotton material, each as wide as your outstretched arms and as long as the distance from your shoulders to your ankles
* scissors
* pencil
* ruler
* needle and thread or glue
* 8 buttons
* piece of cord for a belt

1 Lay the pieces of material on top of each other. In the middle of the top edge, cut an opening for your head about 11 inches wide.

2 Sew or glue the rest of the top edges at intervals a few inches apart. Sew or glue the buttons at intervals along the top edges.

3 Pull the chiton over your head. Wrap the cord around your waist. Pull the chiton up and over the belt until it is the length you want it to be or shorten it by cutting extra material from the bottom edge.

TRY THIS! Add sandals to your look! All you need is a pair of black or white flip-flops and four black or white shoelaces. Tie one end of a shoelace where the top part of the flip-flop is attached to the sole. Repeat on the other side, and then on the other shoe. Next, wrap the laces around and up your legs in crisscross fashion and tie.

PROJECT!

MAKE A BROOCH

SUPPLIES
* newspaper
* small plastic lid, such as the top of a Pringles can
* scissors
* fabric paint, any color
* gold or silver spray paint
* self-sticking brooch pin from the jewelry-making aisle at a craft store or safety pin

Ask an adult to help with the spray paint for this project.

1 Spread the newspaper over your work area. Cut off the edge of the lid. Next, cut the lid to the size you'd like your brooch to be.

2 Use the fabric paint to draw a design on the lid. Ancient Greeks often used **geometric** designs or faces to decorate their jewelry. Let the paint dry completely.

3 When the fabric paint is dry, follow the directions on the spray paint can to paint the lid. Paint both sides if you'd like. Let the spray paint dry.

4 Add the self-sticking pin to the back of your brooch. If you don't have a self-sticking pin, use a safety pin. Just attach it to the back of your brooch with masking tape. You can wear your new brooch on your chiton!

THINK ABOUT IT! Gold was a popular metal for ancient Greek jewelry. It was pretty to look at and **malleable**. What other properties of gold make it useful for things in addition to jewelry?

WORDS TO KNOW

geometric: straight lines and simple shapes such as circles or squares.

malleable: able to be hammered, pressed, or shaped without breaking.

PROJECT!

OLIVE OIL FOOT SCRUB

Ancient Greeks often went barefoot. That could be pretty hard on their feet, so they used olive oil to clean and protect their skin. Here is a simple recipe for making your own foot scrub. This recipe makes enough for one treatment.

SUPPLIES
* small bowl
* spoon
* 2 tablespoons olive oil
* 5 drops of peppermint, spearmint, or wintergreen essential oil (found in the soap-making section of craft stores)
* 1 tablespoon coarse salt

1 Mix the olive oil and the essential oil in your bowl. After they are blended, add the salt. The salt will help scrub off dirt and dead skin.

2 To use your foot scrub, sit on the edge of the bathtub. Rub the scrub all over your bare feet. Keep rubbing for several minutes, until your feet are clean and relaxed. When you're done, rinse your feet with warm soapy water. Dry your feet with a towel completely. Be careful when you're walking on the bathroom floor or other smooth surfaces so you don't slip.

WHAT DID THE SEAMSTRESS SAY AFTER SHE FINISHED MAKING A CHLAMYS?

That's a wrap!

TRY THIS! Do people prefer to go barefoot or wear shoes? Ask your family and friends which they prefer and record their responses in your notebook. Create a graph to show the results. Does the gender or age of the person make a difference in how they answer?

CHAPTER 4
SCHOOL, SOCRATES, AND SCIENCE

The ancient Greeks didn't have school buildings as we do today, but they still believed education was very important. However, their ideas about education were different from what we practice now.

For one thing, not all children were taught mathematics and to read and write. In ancient Greece, girls did not go to school. Their mothers taught them sewing, weaving, cooking, and other household chores at home. However, some wealthy families hired tutors to teach their daughters to read and write.

INVESTIGATE

What subjects were important to ancient Greek students?

SCHOOL, SOCRATES, AND SCIENCE

Poor boys also learned at home. Sometimes, they became apprentices to learn a trade. If a boy's family could afford it, a boy started school when he was about seven. Children went to lessons at a teacher's house or at a public place, such as a market. Learning took place from dawn until dusk.

Younger students learned how to read and write. The teacher who taught these subjects was called a grammatistes. Students didn't have textbooks or calculators as they do today. They read from scrolls, which were long rolls of papyrus. To do math calculations, they used a counter called an abacus.

Ancient Greek boys also learned how to speak in public and debate. Some of their lessons included poetry. They had to memorize poems or parts of poems and recite them by heart.

From about age 12 to 18, physical education took up most of a student's time. To be a good soldier, a boy had to be physically fit, so boys learned to wrestle, box, run, and throw the discus.

WORDS TO KNOW

mathematics: the study of ideas related to numbers. Mathematicians study mathematics.

tutor: a private teacher.

apprentice: someone who learns to do a job by working for someone who already does the job.

grammatistes: an ancient Greek teacher.

scrolls: pieces of papyrus glued together and rolled up.

papyrus: paper made from the papyrus plant.

abacus: an early calculator using beads on rods to add and subtract.

debate: to argue about something, to try to convince the other person of a point of view.

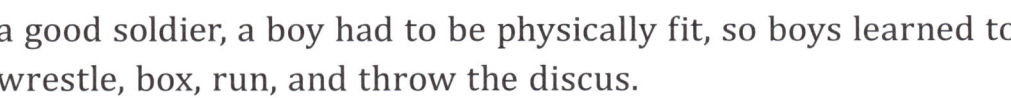

DID YOU KNOW?

Families often hired someone to follow a student to make sure he behaved and worked hard.

GREEKS!

Words to Know

kitharistes: a teacher who taught music in ancient Greece.

lyre: a musical instrument similar to a small harp.

sphere: round, like a ball.

MUSIC

From about age 10 to 12, boys learned to play an instrument from a teacher called a **kitharistes**. Being able to sing and play music was considered an important part of being an educated person. We can't know what ancient Greek music sounded like since no one wrote down songs or music. But by studying vases and other art from that time, we know one of the most popular instruments in ancient Greece was the **lyre**. A lyre looks similar to a miniature harp. It was made using a turtle shell, wooden bows, and three to seven strings for strumming. Drums, finger cymbals, and pipes called aulos (similar to clarinets or oboes) were also popular.

SCIENCE AND MATH

Ancient Greeks were among the first to map the world and the stars. They suggested that the earth was a **sphere**. They were also the first to think that the sun was a ball of fire and that the earth moved around it.

The ancient Greeks also discovered mathematical formulas that we still use. Three important scientists from ancient Greece are Hippocrates, Pythagoras, and Archimedes.

SCHOOL, SOCRATES, AND SCIENCE

> **DID YOU KNOW?**
>
> Doctors take a pledge to do their best and treat patients kindly. This is known as the Hippocratic Oath, named after the ancient Greek scientist Hippocrates.

Hippocrates (460 BCE–370 BCE) was a doctor. In ancient Greece, doctors weren't experts as they are today. However, Hippocrates asked his patients many questions. He kept track of their symptoms and past illnesses. He also helped to write many medical books used by other doctors. Because of all his work, Hippocrates is known as the father of medicine.

Pythagoras (c. 569 BCE–c. 500 BCE) was one of the first mathematicians. He studied numbers and patterns. Some of his greatest discoveries had to do with triangles.

Archimedes (287 BCE–212 BCE) was a mathematician and inventor. The Archimedes' screw was one of his inventions. It was a simple machine that used a turning motion to move water from one place to another.

CREDIT: WELLCOME COLLECTION (CC BY 4.0)

Archimedes' screws are still in use today! **Check out this video.**

🔍 ARCHIMEDEAN SCREW IN ACTION

43

GREEKS!

> **philosopher:** a person who studies knowledge, truth, and the nature of reality.
>
> **WORDS TO KNOW**

PHILOSOPHY

Ancient Greeks were very interested in philosophy. People who study philosophy are called **philosophers**. They consider big ideas. For example, they think about right and wrong. They examine beauty, religion, and nature. Ancient Greece is known for its philosophers, especially Socrates, Plato, and Aristotle.

Socrates (c. 470 BCE–399 BCE) was a teacher who believed knowledge should be free. He didn't charge for teaching, and he loved to challenge his students. He would ask a question, listen to the response, and then keep asking questions and listening until the student arrived at the truth. For example, someone might say, "The sky is always blue." And Socrates might ask, "What about when it rains?" or "What about at night?" This back-and-forth questioning is called the Socratic method.

IT'S ALL GREEK TO ME!

The Greek alphabet has 24 letters. It is based on the alphabet of the Phoenicians, neighbors of the ancient Greeks. The Greek alphabet is considered the first real alphabet because it was the first to use symbols for each vowel and consonant sound. The ancient alphabet is still used in modern-day Greece. Many Greek words are roots of English words. For example: *bibl-* means "book" and is the root of bible and bibliography. And many of the Greek letters are used in science and mathematics, too. Here are some common Greek letters that are used in science and math.

ε Epsilon Δ Delta α Alpha π Pi

SCHOOL, SOCRATES, AND SCIENCE

WHY WAS THE MATH SCROLL STRESSED OUT?

It had too many problems.

Athens's leaders grew upset with Socrates because they thought he didn't respect the gods. When he was 70, Socrates was arrested and sentenced to death.

Plato (c. 428 BCE–348 BCE) was one of Socrates's followers. After Socrates died, Plato wrote down Socrates's ideas and the conversations the two of them had. This was fortunate, since Socrates didn't write anything himself! Plato was interested in learning what makes people act the way they do. He also wondered if something is real only because we believe it's real.

A FAMOUS 1511 PAINTING CALLED *SCHOOL OF ATHENS* BY RENAISSANCE PAINTER RAPHAEL SHOWS PLATO AND ARISTOTLE WALKING TOGETHER.

GREEKS!

> **WORDS TO KNOW**
>
> **knucklebones:** a game where players tossed small bones into the air and tried to catch them.

Aristotle (384 BCE–322 BCE) was one of Plato's students. He used philosophy to study nature and the ways of the world. His greatest contribution was his practical method of figuring things out. Because of this, Aristotle is known as the father of the scientific method. You can learn about the scientific method on page 7!

FUN AND GAMES

Ancient Greek children didn't spend all their time studying and doing sports. They played, too. Many of their toys were similar to the toys we have today. They played with balls, hoops that they rolled along the ground, tops, dolls made of clay, yo-yos, and models of animals. They also had board games such as backgammon and chess. Girls often played **knucklebones**, which is a lot like the game of jacks.

When children became teenagers, they were considered grown up. To show they had really left behind their childhoods, they had to give away all their toys. Do you think that happens in today's world?

Another way people had fun was by going to the theater and attending the Olympics! We'll learn more about these in the next chapter.

CONSIDER AND DISCUSS

It's time to consider and discuss: What subjects were important to ancient Greek students?

PROJECT!

POETRY SCROLL

Ancient Greeks who read poetry out loud to entertain others were called bards. Once you finish this project, you can dress up in a chiton and be a bard!

> **SUPPLIES**
> * newspaper
> * 3 pieces of white paper, 8½ by 11 inches
> * baking sheet or shallow tray
> * ½ cup cold coffee or tea
> * wax paper
> * tape (clear or masking)
> * poem (pick a favorite or write your own)
> * marker

1 Cover your workspace with newspaper. Place the three pieces of white paper into the baking sheet or shallow tray. Slowly pour the cold coffee or tea over the paper. Let the paper soak for five minutes.

2 Carefully lift each piece of paper, letting the extra liquid drip off. Without stacking them, lay the sheets on wax paper to dry.

3 When the sheets of paper are completely dry, tape them together lengthwise. To complete your scroll, write your poem on the middle page.

> **DID YOU KNOW?**
>
> Ancient Greek students wrote on a wooden tablet that was covered in wax. They etched their letters and numbers into the wax using a long stick called a stylus. The stylus had a flat end to rub out mistakes.

4 Roll the paper from both ends to the middle. When you're done, your paper will look like an ancient Greek scroll. To recite your poem, gently unroll the scroll and start reading.

> **THINK ABOUT IT!** How is paper made today? What materials do we use?

PROJECT!

PUMP IT UP!

Archimedes screws were an important invention because they allowed ancient Greeks to easily move water. We still use Archimedes screws today.

SUPPLIES
* 2 feet of half-inch PVC pipe
* 4 feet clear, plastic tubing, about half-inch inner diameter
* duct tape
* water
* food coloring (any color)
* spoon
* 2 bowls
* a way to raise one of the bowls (for example, an old book or small box)

1 Use a piece of tape to secure one end of the tubing to one end of the pipe. Make sure to leave about 1 inch of extra tubing hanging off the end.

2 Wrap the rest of the tubing around the pipe at intervals about 2 inches apart. Add a few pieces of tape to keep the tubing in place along the pipe if you'd like.

3 When you're done wrapping, tape the tubing to the pipe. Make sure to leave about an inch of extra tubing hanging off at this end, too.

4 Fill the bowls about halfway with water. Add a few drops of food coloring to the first bowl and mix.

5 Place one of the bowls on the table. Place the second bowl on top of the book or box. The bowls should be about 2 feet apart in distance. (The ends of your 2-foot long PVC pipe will each rest over a bowl.)

PROJECT!

ANCIENT GREEK STORIES

In the ninth or eight century BCE, a man named **Homer** recited two **epic** poems that we still read today—the *Iliad* and the *Odyssey*. The *Iliad* retells the story of the Trojan War. The *Odyssey* tells the story of Odysseus, a war hero, and his journey home from the Trojan War. The *Odyssey* has more than 12,000 lines, and the *Iliad* has more than 15,000 lines!

6 To use your Archimedes screw, place one end of the pipe in the lower bowl at a low angle and gently turn a few times. The angle depends on how high your other bowl is. The extra tubing at the end should scoop up a tiny bit of water.

7 Keep turning the pipe so it can scoop up more water. What's happening to the water inside the tubing? This might take a few minutes, so be patient. When the water is near the top, be sure to have the second bowl ready!

THINK ABOUT IT! What do you think would happen if you used plastic tubing with a bigger diameter? Would the water move faster or slower or the same as before? Try it and see.

WORDS TO KNOW

Homer: a famous ancient Greek poet who created the *Iliad* and the *Odyssey*.

epic: a long poem that tells of the deeds of a legendary hero.

PROJECT!

KNUCKLEBONES

Knucklebones was a game the ancient Romans played. They used real animal bones, but you can make your own from air-dry clay.

SUPPLIES
* ¾ cup white school glue
* 1 cup cornstarch
* 2 teaspoons baby oil
* 2 teaspoons lemon juice
* small saucepan
* wooden spoon
* stove

Note: Ask an adult to help with the stove.

1 Combine glue, cornstarch, baby oil, and lemon juice in the saucepan. Place the pan on the stove and stir continually on low-medium heat for five to 10 minutes. The consistency should go from liquid to a dough.

2 Remove the pan from the stove. Knead the dough for two to three minutes on a flat surface. It will be warm, so be careful not to burn yourself. The dough should be smooth and soft.

3 Divide and roll the dough into five balls. Pinch and shape the balls to look like knucklebones. Let your "knucklebones" dry for a day.

To Play:

* Sitting on a flat surface, gently toss the five knucklebones in front of you. Pick one up to be your "jack." Hold the jack in the palm of your hand. Toss it in the air. While the jack is in the air, use the same hand to scoop up one knucklebone and then catch the jack before it lands. Toss the jack again, only this time, scoop up two knucklebones before the jack can land. For the next turn, scoop three knucklebones, then all four at a time. The object is to get through all stages without dropping the jack or missing any of the knucklebones.

TRY THIS! Play with a friend. Toss, gather, and catch until you miss the jack or the correct number of knucklebones. When this happens, it's your friend's turn.

CHAPTER 5
THE OLYMPICS AND THEATER

Because soldiers in ancient Greece often had to fight hand-to-hand, sports were a way to train for war. Being a fast runner or good boxer came in handy on the battlefield. Sports contests were a way of showing off fighting skills and proving to the public that an army was strong.

Many city-states held regular sports contests during religious festivals. For example, Athens had an event called the Panathenaic Games. These games were held during the festival to honor Athena, the goddess of wisdom and protector of Athens.

? INVESTIGATE

How are the modern Olympics different from the ancient Olympics?

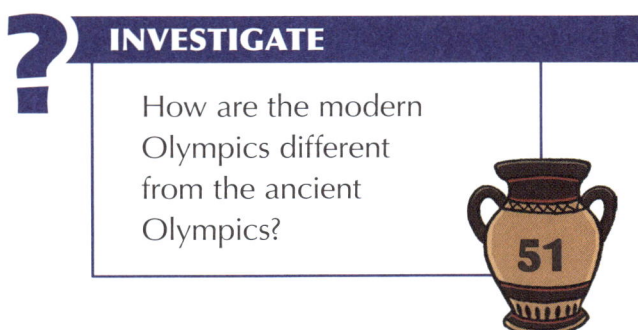

GREEKS!

> **goddess:** a female god.
>
> **Olympics:** the most popular sports contest in ancient Greece, now a global event held every four years.
>
> **WORDS TO KNOW**

THE OLYMPICS

The most popular sports contest in ancient Greece was the Olympics. Do you watch the Olympic Games, when the world's countries come together to compete in different sports? We got the Olympics from ancient Greece.

The first Olympic games were held in 776 BCE in the city-state of Olympia, in southern Greece. The games were part of a festival that honored the god Zeus. As with the modern Olympics, the ancient games were held every four years. Men and boys traveled from all around Greece to compete. Foreigners and women were not allowed to compete.

AN ANCIENT LIST OF OLYMPIC VICTORS ON PAPYRUS

> **DID YOU KNOW?**
>
> The ancient Olympic games were so popular, Olympia usually wasn't prepared for the crowds. There wasn't enough water for the guests. People camped out and went to the bathroom outside and many fainted from the heat and lack of water!

THE OLYMPICS AND THEATER

Heraia: an Olympic-style competition for women.

WORDS TO KNOW

Married women were not even allowed to watch the games! This is because the athletes were naked. No one knows for certain why they didn't wear clothes while competing. One theory is that it was for safety. According to legend, an athlete's pants had once fallen down while he was running. He tripped, hit his head, and died.

The more likely explanation is that the ancient Greeks simply liked to show off how fit they were. Plus, it was very hot. To enhance their muscles and to protect their skin from the sun, athletes covered themselves with olive oil.

People from as far away as Egypt came to admire the athletes' skills. The stadium in Olympia held more than 40,000 spectators, and even more people came to sneak a peek or just be part of the five-day celebration. Greeks believed everyone should make the journey to see the games at least once in their lives.

WHAT DID THE WINNER OF THE OLYMPIC RACE LOSE?

His breath!

CHEER ON THE WOMEN

Greek women had their own Olympic-style competition. These games were called the **Heraia**. They were a series of footraces held in honor of the goddess Hera. They took place every four years at the same stadium as the Olympics. However, women did not compete naked—they wore tunics that fell to their knees.

GREEKS!

> **pentathlon:** an Olympic event that includes five sports. In ancient times, the contests included discus and javelin throwing, running, long jumping, and wrestling.
>
> **pankration:** a brutal sport of the ancient Greek Olympics that combined boxing and wrestling.
>
> **WORDS TO KNOW**

AND THEY'RE OFF!

Many of the ancient Olympic games are ones we're familiar with today—boxing, wrestling, horse racing, discus and javelin throwing, and long jumping. Plus, footraces! These sprints were the most popular sport.

The games also included a **pentathlon**, which means "five contests." The ancient Greek pentathlon included discus throwing, javelin throwing, running, long jumping, and wrestling. Today, pentathlons include long-distance running, swimming, target shooting, fencing, and horseback riding.

DID YOU KNOW?

Wars were temporarily stopped so people could travel to the games. Although wars don't stop for the Olympic games today, countries often set aside their differences and try to get along while competing.

Another popular event was the **pankration**, which combined boxing and wrestling and was a little like what we now call ultimate fighting. Fighters could do just about anything they wanted to their opponents. The only rule was no gouging the other person's eyes.

THE OLYMPICS AND THEATER

As you can imagine, pankration was a dangerous sport. Many fighters died rather than give up.

> **laurel:** a wreath made of olive leaves that Olympic winners wore on their heads.

WORDS TO KNOW

Today, Olympic athletes win gold, silver, and bronze medals. In ancient times, athletes won **laurels** made of olive tree leaves. Sometimes, they won a piece of pottery or the discus they had thrown.

Different countries host the Olympic Games. During the opening ceremonies, the host country gets to show off its history and culture. **Take a look at this video of opening ceremonies from the 1908 games to the 2012 games.** The 1980 Moscow games are not included, most likely because many countries skipped these games in protest of Russia's invasion of Afghanistan.

🔍 OLYMPIC OPENING CEREMONIES JOURNEY

Like many modern Olympians, ancient athletes enjoyed plenty of glory in their hometowns. They received gifts and free meals and were treated as heroes for the rest of their lives. It's not surprising so many athletes trained and made the long journey to the Olympics to compete.

SAVING THE OLYMPICS

The ancient Greeks held the Olympics until 393 CE. When the Romans took over Greece, they banned the Olympics because the games worshipped ancient Greek gods. The Olympics could have been lost forever if it wasn't for the French baron Pierre de Coubertin (1863–1937). Inspired by the spirit of competition of the ancient games, he helped organize the first modern-day Olympics, held in Athens in 1896 CE.

GREEKS!

> **WORDS TO KNOW**
>
> **tiers:** rows arranged one above another.
>
> **orchestra:** an area in front of the stage where the chorus performed in ancient Greek plays.

BROADWAY!

The theater was another popular form of entertainment in ancient Greece. As with the Olympics, plays began as part of religious festivals. Soon, though, ancient Greeks began putting on plays all the time. They even had contests to see who could write the best play.

Plays took place in large theaters built in a half-circle shape, so the sound carried well. A theater was often carved into the side of a hill or mountain. **Tiers** of stone seats faced the stage. The chorus performed on a flat, round area called the **orchestra** in front of the stage.

> **DID YOU KNOW?**
>
> Ancient Greek theater masks often had two sides so an actor could change emotions quickly.

THE OLYMPICS AND THEATER

The chorus was a group of dancers, musicians, and singers who helped explain the play to the audience. They were similar to narrators. Outside the theater, vendors sold food, drinks, and cushions for the stone seats.

Though women could go to plays, they couldn't act in them. Men played all of the parts. The actors wore costumes and masks made with stiff cloth, which had exaggerated features the audience could see more clearly. Some theaters could seat more than 12,000 people—imagine having a seat far from the stage! The masks helped the audience know who the character was and how they were feeling.

> **narrator:** someone who tells or helps tell a story.
>
> **exaggerate:** to make something sound larger, greater, better, or worse than it really is.
>
> **comedy:** a funny play.
>
> **tragedy:** a sad play.
>
> **myth:** a traditional story dealing with ancestors or heroes or even supernatural figures.
>
> **satire:** plays that poke fun at leaders or serious issues.
>
> **WORDS TO KNOW**

 CONSIDER AND DISCUSS

It's time to consider and discuss: How are the modern Olympics different from the ancient Olympics?

The most popular plays were comedies and tragedies. Comedies were usually about ordinary people in funny situations. Tragedies were sad plays. They were usually about Greek myths or gods and goddesses. Satires were also popular. These plays poked fun at leaders or serious issues.

What else besides the Olympics theater did the modern world gain from ancient Greece? How about a whole style of government? We'll learn about that in the next chapter.

PROJECT!

MAKE A LAUREL WREATH

SUPPLIES
* 6 green pipe cleaners
* scissors
* 1 or 2 packages of silk leaves with wire stems, from a craft store

A laurel wreath is a sign of victory. In ancient Greece, Olympic winners received wreaths made from olive tree leaves.

1 Make a headband out of pipe cleaners. Twist two pipe cleaners together to make one strong piece. Do this a total of three times. Then twist the ends of the three lengths of pipe cleaner together to make one long piece.

2 Wrap the pipe cleaner around your head. The band should be snug. Be sure you can put it on and take it off easily.

3 Once you have the right size circle, tie off the ends of the twisted pipe cleaners and trim any extra.

4 Making sure all the leaves are going in the same direction, attach them to the headband by wrapping the stem wires around the pipe cleaner headband.

5 Keep adding leaves until you've gone all around the headband. Add as many leaves as you want. Wear your wreath!

THINK ABOUT IT! Olympic gold medals used to be made of 100-percent gold. Today, only a small percentage of the medals are gold. The silver and bronze medals are not made with solid metal either. In 2016, the Rio Summer Games used eco-friendly medals (by removing mercury) and recycled ribbons. Can you think of other ways the Olympics could be earth-friendly?

PROJECT!

LONG-JUMP CONTEST

The first Olympics including long jumping as part of the pentathlon. The other pentathlon events included discus throwing, javelin throwing, running, and wrestling. You and your friends can hold your own long-jump contest.

SUPPLIES
* friends
* 3 jump ropes
* tape measure
* large, soft space to jump (such as a sand pit or grassy area)
* craft sticks
* markers

1 Have everyone who is jumping write their name on a craft stick using the marker. You can decorate the sticks if you'd like, too!

2 Lay two of the jump ropes parallel to each other. They should be 4 feet apart. This will be your jumping area.

3 Lay the other rope at one end of the ropes to create a starting line. (You can fold the rope to fit in between the two parallel ropes.)

4 The first jumper should stand with their feet behind the starting line. When they are ready, the jumper jumps as far as they can and lands with their feet together. Try to bend your knees, spring forward, and bend your knees again to land. The jumper can take three jumps. He or she marks the longest jump using their craft stick. Plant the name markers on the outside of the jumping area to make sure no one gets hurts.

5 Each jumper takes a turn. Use the markers or tape measure to determine who had the longest jump.

TRY THIS! The person with the longest jump can wear the laurel wreath you made on page 58. Or you and your friends can create your own versions of Olympic medals for first, second, and third place.

PROJECT!

THEATER MASK

Take a bow and be an actor with your own mask!

SUPPLIES
* newspaper
* foil
* scissors
* plaster bandage wrap (found in craft stores)
* bowl of water
* sandpaper (optional)
* acrylic paint
* yarn or fake hair (optional)
* heavy string

1 Decide on the emotion you want your mask to show. Sketch your idea in your field notebook.

2 Spread newspaper on your work area. Crumple up some newspaper into an oval face shape and lay the foil on top. Pinch the foil or mold or roll foil pieces to create features such as a nose or chin. You can also place the foil over your own face to get a general shape. Then, use newspaper underneath to support it.

3 Cut the plaster bandages into strips about 6 inches long. Also cut some smaller pieces.

4 Dip the plaster bandage strips into the water and gently lay them on top of the foil. Keep adding strips and smaller pieces to create a face, leaving eye and mouth holes. Think about the emotion you're trying to convey. For example, a surprised face might have raised eyebrows and a rounded mouth. A sad face might have a frown.

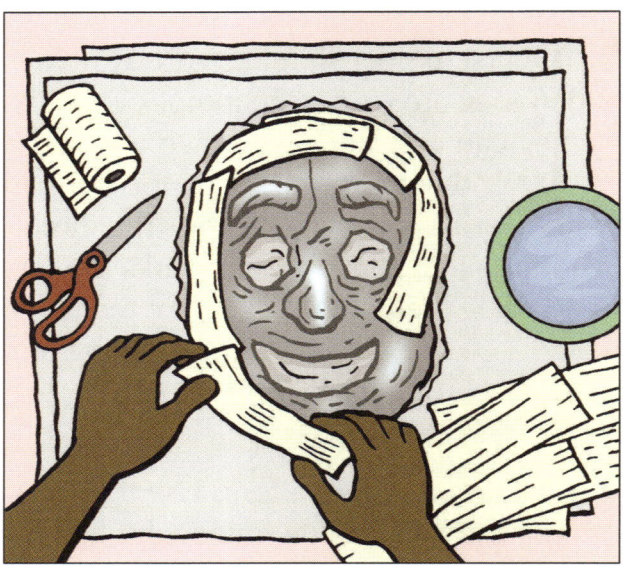

PROJECT!

5 Let the mask dry completely. Once dry, trim the sides to make them smooth or use sandpaper to smooth out rough edges. Paint the mask. When the paint is dry, glue on fake hair (or yarn for hair) if you want.

6 Poke holes in the sides of the mask and tie two pieces of string about 12 inches long through each hole so you can tie the mask to your face.

THINK ABOUT IT! Phidias (480 BCE–430 BCE) was an ancient Greek sculptor and mathematician who supposedly used a mathematical formula when creating statues of men, women, and gods. This formula, called the golden ratio, says a beautiful person's face will be approximately 1.6 times longer than it is wide. Do you think this idea has any truth? Or is beauty, as the saying goes, in the eye of the beholder?

THIS SHAPE IS CALLED THE FIBONACCI SPIRAL OR THE GOLDEN SPIRAL, AND IT FOLLOWS THE SAME MATHEMATICAL DESIGN AS THE GOLDEN RATIO.

CHAPTER 6
DEMOCRACY AND WAR

Do you ever listen to world leaders give speeches? Do you follow elections when they happen? Governments in which the people have a say are called democracies. And guess who invented democracy? The ancient Greeks!

Early in the history of ancient Greece, kings ruled the city-states. Later, a small group of wealthy people ruled. But in Athens, something special happened around 508 BCE. People came up with a new way to run things—a form of government called a democracy.

INVESTIGATE

How is ancient Greek democracy different from today's democracy?

DEMOCRACY AND WAR

THE PEOPLE'S RULE

> **Assembly:** a group of 6,000 citizens in ancient Greece who met, discussed, and then voted on important matters in Athens.
>
> **citizen:** a member of a city or country who enjoys certain rights.
>
> **Council:** a group of 500 ancient Greeks who made laws and chose military leaders.
>
> **WORDS to KNOW**

The word *democracy* means "people's rule." The main feature of Athens's democracy was the Assembly. It was similar to a town meeting. Any citizen could be a part of the Assembly—but only free men who were born in Athens were considered citizens.

In the Assembly, citizens voiced their opinions and voted on big decisions, such as whether or not to go to war. The people in the Assembly voted by raising their hands. The side with the most votes won.

A smaller group of 500 members within the Assembly was called the Council. They handled day-to-day issues such as making laws and creating policies. They took turns meeting—50 members at a time met at a round building called the Tholos. Council members were chosen from the Assembly and served on the Council for one year.

PYNX HILL IN ATHENS, WHERE CITIZENS FIRST GATHERED FOR ASSEMBLIES
CREDIT: LARRY (CC BY 2.0)

GREEKS!

juror: someone who is part of a jury.

jury: a group of people who hear a case in court. Jurors give their opinion, called a verdict.

WORDS TO KNOW

LAW AND ORDER

Ancient Greek citizens had to serve as jurors every once in a while. Ancient Greeks thought sitting on a jury was exciting.

Jurors were at least 30 years old and citizens of Athens. They were picked at random. Juries were usually large, with 200 to 500 members. This made it harder for the accused to pay jurors to vote in his favor and a tie was rare.

DID YOU KNOW?

Ancient Greek juries had hundreds of people. Today, in the United States, juries have 12 people.

The person accused of a crime made a speech to tell his side of the story. When he was done, the jury voted using small bronze tokens. A "guilty" token had a hole in the middle of it. An "innocent" token had no hole. All of the tokens went into a clay jar and were counted.

In Athens, punishment didn't usually mean jail. Some guilty people had to pay a fine. Others lost their rights or some of their possessions. Jail was saved for people who committed serious crimes, such as murder.

DEMOCRACY AND WAR

FIGHTING

cavalry: soldiers on horseback.
hoplite: a Greek foot soldier.
torso: the human body except the head, arms, and legs.

WORDS TO KNOW

Ancient Greece had many city-states that didn't always get along. To protect themselves, the people of Athens built a strong army. This army included soldiers on horses, called the cavalry. Other soldiers included stone throwers and archers. The backbone of Athens's army was its foot soldiers, called hoplites.

Hoplites started their two-year training at age 18. They were not paid and even had to provide their own weapons and armor. They carried round shields made of bronze or leather and wore helmets that often had crests made of animal hair. Some helmets had a plate to cover the soldier's nose or long sides to cover his cheeks. Other helmets had holes for a soldier's mouth or ears.

Hoplites used bronze breastplates to protect their torsos. These breastplates were made especially for the wearer. They had two sides—one covered the front of the body and one protected the back.

WHAT DO YOU CALL THE MILITARY LEADER WHO MISSED THE BATTLE BECAUSE HE OVERSLEPT?

Alexander the Late!

A GREEK HOPLITE FIGHTING A PERSIAN SOLDIER

GREEKS!

> **greaves:** a piece of armor used to protect the shin.
>
> **Persian Empire:** an ancient empire to the south and east of Greece.
>
> **WORDS TO KNOW**

 Forming a shape called the phalanx formation was an effective tool for the ancient Greek army. **Take a look!**

🔎 **SEE U PHALANX**

The fronts of a soldier's legs, from the knee to the ankle, were protected by **greaves**, which looked similar to the shin guards that soccer players wear. Hoplites sometimes carried short swords into battle, but their main weapon was a long spear.

We've seen gods and goddesses mentioned in this book. Let's take a closer look at them in the next chapter.

ALEXANDER THE GREAT

One of ancient Greece's best military leaders was Alexander the Great (356 BCE–323 BCE). The son of a powerful king named Phillip II of Macedonia (382 BCE–336 BCE), Alexander took over when he was just 20 years old. During the next 11 years, Alexander led his large and powerful army over thousands of miles, invading many lands, including the **Persian Empire**. Alexander conquered the entire world known in ancient times! Legend says that he never lost a battle. Alexander also worked to blend the cultures of the lands he conquered. He encouraged his soldiers to marry women there. His actions helped to bring about a peaceful period of history for ancient Greece. The city of Alexandria, Egypt, was named after Alexander the Great.

? CONSIDER AND DISCUSS

It's time to consider and discuss: How is ancient Greek democracy different from today's democracy?

PROJECT!

JURY TOKENS

Need to take a vote? Make your own jury tokens!

SUPPLIES
- ½ cup fine sawdust from a hardware store with bits of wood or splinters removed
- ¼ cup flour
- bowl
- water
- wax paper
- butter knife
- bronze acrylic paint

1 Use your hands to combine the sawdust and flour in the bowl. Slowly add a little water. Knead the dough until it is stiff. Keep kneading until the dough has a stretchy feel to it.

2 Dump the dough onto a piece of wax paper. Roll and pat the dough into a disc that is about the size of a half-dollar and about a quarter-inch thick. Use the knife to cut the dough if you want. This will be your "not guilty" token.

3 Make another disc. Use the knife to carefully cut a hole in the center of this token. This will be your "guilty" token.

4 Let the tokens dry completely. When they're dry, paint them.

TRY THIS! Instead of making "guilty" and "not guilty" tokens, make them "yes" and "no" tokens. Give everyone in your family or classroom one so they can vote on a common decision. For example, "Should we have pizza for dinner?" Instead of just counting the tokens, create a simple bar graph to show which choice got more votes.

PROJECT!

MAKE A WATER CLOCK

Ancient Greeks kept track of time during trials and government proceedings by using a water clock that worked with simple clay pots. Here is an easy way to make your own water clock using modern materials.

SUPPLIES
* 2 plastic containers, one smaller than the other
* pointy scissors
* ruler
* duct tape
* measuring cup
* water
* timer

Note: Ask an adult for help with the pointy scissors.

1 Set the larger of the two containers on a flat surface. Tape the ruler on the back side of the container so the ruler is **vertical**.

2 Use the pointy scissors to poke a very small hole in the middle of the bottom of the smaller container. The hole should allow water to drip out steadily, but not pour out. To test this, add some water to the container and hold it over a sink. If the water drips out too slowly, make the hole a little bit bigger. If the water pours out, make the hole smaller by putting a piece of duct tape over part of the hole.

3 After you get the drip hole just right, tape the small container to the top of the ruler, directly above the larger container

4 Pour ¼ cup of water into the top container. Start the timer. How long does it take for all of the water to drip into the larger container?

5 Try experimenting with more or less water to see if you can get your water clock to keep time for one minute, then two minutes, then five minutes.

THINK ABOUT IT!
What are other ways ancient people marked the passage of time? (Hint: One of them used the sun.)

WORDS TO KNOW

vertical: straight up and down.

PROJECT!

DEFEND YOURSELF!

SUPPORTS
- large piece of thick cardboard
- ruler
- scissors
- markers or paint
- brown duct tape

The shields that hoplites used were typically 31 to 39 inches in diameter and weighed 14 to 18 pounds. Don't worry, yours won't weight that much!

1 Cut the cardboard into a circle with a diameter of 18 inches.

2 On one side of the cardboard, use the markers or paint to create your own shield design. The ancient Greeks got to design their own shields, too. When your design is finished, turn the cardboard over.

3 Tear or cut two strips of duct tape that are each 10 inches long. Lay one piece, sticky-side-up, on a flat surface. Carefully lay the second strip on top of it, sticky-side-down. This is your shield's handle.

YOU CAN SEE A HOPLITE ON THE EDGE OF THIS LARGE BOWL, FOUND IN MODERN-DAY FRANCE IN 1953.

4 Lay your handle in the center of the back of the shield. Use more duct tape to secure each end to the shield. Be sure not to lay the handle completely flat—you need to be able to slip your arm through it. Now you're ready to fight ancient-Greek style.

THINK ABOUT IT! Is this shield similar to ones that other cultures used in the past? Why is the shape, weight, and design of a shield important?

CHAPTER 7
GODS, GODDESSES, AND MYTHS

You might think that religion wasn't important to ancient Greeks. They didn't have churches, holy books, or religious leaders. But, in fact, religion was part of their everyday lives. Their gods and goddesses were on the minds of ancient Greeks no matter what they were doing!

Ancient Greeks didn't believe in one god. They believed in many gods. These included the 12 main ones, sometimes called the Olympian gods, who were thought to live on **Mount Olympus**.

> **? INVESTIGATE**
>
> How did religion play a part in the lives of ancient Greeks?

GODS, GODDESSES, AND MYTHS

The ancient Greeks believed their gods were a lot like people. They fell in love, married, had kids, grew angry and jealous, and enjoyed music and dancing. The ancient Greeks also believed the gods were involved with people's everyday lives and controlled events such as the weather and illnesses.

> **WORDS TO KNOW**
>
> **Mount Olympus:** the mountain where the ancient Greek gods lived.
>
> **altar:** a raised table for religious ceremonies.
>
> **votive:** something that is a symbol for a wish.
>
> **oracle:** a woman in ancient Greece who supposedly spoke for the gods and offered advice.

Ancient Greeks worshipped gods and goddesses at festivals throughout the year. They also worshipped at home. Every home had an **altar** in its courtyard, where household members left offerings, such as food, gold, or silver, for the gods. When they were ill or hurt and wanted a god to help them, ancient Greeks left **votives**, or models of the body part that needed healing.

Though they didn't have official religious leaders, the ancient Greeks did have **oracles**, or women who were thought to speak for the gods. Ancient Greeks visited oracles for advice about all kinds of things. Sometimes, their advice was good. But most of their advice was too vague to be helpful.

A STATUE OF ZEUS, KING OF GODS

GREEKS!

> **underworld:** in Greek mythology, the place beneath the earth where people believed the souls of the dead went.
>
> **WORDS TO KNOW**

STORYTIME

Myths are stories that teach a lesson or explain how something in the world came to be. There are hundreds of Greeks myths, and gods and goddesses play a part in many of them. You'll find many Greek myths to be very familiar. Have you heard about King Midas? What about Achilles?

Midas was a peasant made into a king by the gods. King Midas thought nothing in the world was more important than money. When the god Dionysus granted him a wish, King Midas wished that everything he touched would turn to gold.

OLYMPIAN GODS

Zeus: King of the gods and god of the sky, thunder, and lightning.

Hera: Zeus's wife and goddess of women and marriage.

Apollo: God of music and fortune-telling and Artemis's twin.

Artemis: Goddess of nature and Apollo's twin.

Athena: Goddess of wisdom.

Ares: God of war.

Aphrodite: Goddess of love and beauty.

Demeter: Goddess of grain and the harvest.

Hades: God of the underworld.

Hermes: Messenger of the gods who also took the dead to the underworld.

Hephaestus: God of fire.

Poseidon: God of the sea.

GODS, GODDESSES, AND MYTHS

At first, Midas loved his gift. But when he grew hungry, the food he touched turned to gold. When Midas accidentally turned his daughter into gold, he was terribly sad. He begged Dionysus to undo the wish. Dionysus told King Midas to bathe in the Pactolus River. For this reason—according to the myth—that river's bank had lots of gold in ancient times.

> **WORDS TO KNOW**
> **tendon:** tissue that connects muscles to bones.

> **DID YOU KNOW?**
> The tendon that connects your heel bone to your calf muscles is called the Achilles tendon after the myth of Achilles!

Achilles was the son of a fairy. His mother worried about her son's safety. To protect her baby, she dipped him in the River Styx, which was supposed to make him impossible to kill. But, she held the baby by the heel when she dunked him in the water.

Achilles grew up and become a great soldier. During the Trojan War, someone shot a poisoned arrow into Achilles's heel and he died. The lesson of the story of Achilles is that everyone has a weakness.

THETIS DIPPING THE INFANT ACHILLES INTO THE RIVER STYX, PAINTED AROUND 1630 AND 1635
CREDIT: PETER PAUL REUBENS

GREEKS!

THE TROJAN WAR

Maybe you've heard of the Trojan War, one of the most famous wars of all time. But, we don't know for sure whether it really took place!

The storyteller Homer tells us about the war in his epic poem, the *Iliad*. The city of Troy, where the war took place, might have been real. Some people believe the Trojan War might have been several real wars whose tales got mixed together. But, whether it was real or not, the Trojan War is a great story.

WHAT WOULD BE A GOOD NICKNAME FOR THE GREEK SOLDIERS WHO HID INSIDE THE TROJAN HORSE?

The Horse Force!

According to Homer, the war started when a few goddesses argued about who was the most beautiful. Zeus sent a Trojan man named Paris to settle the argument. Paris picked the goddess Aphrodite. As a reward, Aphrodite promised Paris he could marry any woman he wanted.

Paris wanted Helen, said to be the most beautiful woman in the world. The only problem was that Helen was already married to a Greek man named Menelaus. He wasn't happy when Helen and Paris ran away together. Menelaus and his allies banded together to get her back, and the Trojan War began.

> **DID YOU KNOW?**
> In the late 1800s, a German archaeologist named Heinrich Schliemann (1822–1890) found what might be the remains of Troy in Turkey.

GODS, GODDESSES, AND MYTHS

For 10 years, the Trojans and Greeks battled, while different gods and goddesses took sides and intervened. For example, Apollo sent a **plague** to the Greek camp.

> **plague:** a serious disease that spreads quickly to many people and often causes death.
>
> **surrender:** to admit defeat and give up.
>
> **WORDS TO KNOW**

In the end, the Greeks defeated the Trojans in a very sneaky way. First, they built a large wooden horse. Then, they pretended to **surrender** and left the horse as a gift outside the walls of Troy. The Trojans, not knowing that Greek soldiers were hiding inside the horse, brought it into the city. That night, the Greek soldiers snuck out of the horse. The Trojans were caught by surprise and had no choice but to surrender.

 Many works of art imagine what the Trojan Horse looked like. **Here's an engraving you can find at the Smithsonian American Art Museum by artist Roderick Mead.**

🔎 SAAM TROJAN MEAD →

75

GREEKS!

frieze: a narrow, horizontal, decorative panel.

Ionic column: a simple Greek column with a scroll-like top.

Corinthian column: a Greek column with an elaborate, leafy top.

WORDS TO KNOW

TEMPLES

One way we know that gods and goddesses were important to ancient Greeks is through the temples they built in honor of those gods and goddesses. Ancient Greek temples were the gods' and goddesses' homes.

Temples were often made from marble or limestone and had fancy tile roofs. Many of them had columns and large statues of the gods. Beautiful bands of carved scenes, called **friezes**, decorated the outsides of temples.

DID YOU KNOW?

Many temples served as storage areas for valuables. Ancient Greeks believed no one would rob a god's home.

GREEK COLUMNS

The columns of the Parthenon are Doric columns. They have thick bottoms and plain tops. This was a very common column style in ancient Greece. **Ionic columns** were also common. These had fancy, scroll-like tops. **Corinthian columns** were a little less common. These columns had elaborate, leafy tops.

GODS, GODDESSES, AND MYTHS

The most famous and grandest of all ancient Greek temples is the Parthenon. It was dedicated to the goddess Athena and completed on Athens's acropolis in 423 BCE. Like most temples, it was a rectangular building with a triangular roof. It was much bigger than most temples, though, nearly 240 feet long, 110 feet wide, and 60 feet tall. There were eight columns on each end and 17 columns along each side.

The Parthenon was made of marble and had wooden beams that supported the marble ceiling. A splendid, 45-foot-tall ivory statue of Athena stood inside. Precious jewels were used for the eyes and thin pieces of gold for the clothes. It took 15 years to build the Parthenon, which stood as a great symbol of Athens's beauty and power.

Throughout history, fire, war, and invasions took their toll on the magnificent building. Fortunately, part of it remains for us to see today.

THE PARTHENON

GREEKS!

FERRY TOLL

Ancient Greeks believed that when people died, their souls journeyed to the River Styx, the river between Earth and the underworld. There, a god ferried them across the river to be judged. Since the ferry captain had to be paid, families put a coin inside a dead person's pocket. Coins were first made in ancient Greece around 600 BCE. They were made from silver and gold and called a drachma. It was one of the earliest coins in the world. Each city-state had its own coins.

DID YOU KNOW?

Have you ever heard of a computer virus called the Trojan Horse? Why do you think it's named that?

The height of ancient Greek civilization lasted for about 350 years, from 800-31 BCE. During those years, ancient Greece was home to some of the greatest philosophers, storytellers, and soldiers in the world. We also have ancient Greeks to thank for the Olympic Games and democracy! Their cities were beautiful and many of their temples, such as the Parthenon, are still around for us to enjoy and learn from.

Maybe someday you'll visit modern-day Greece or visit a museum and discover the artifacts from this great, ancient civilization yourself!

CONSIDER AND DISCUSS

It's time to consider and discuss: How did religion play a part in the lives of ancient Greeks?

PROJECT!

POST-AND-LINTEL EXPERIMENT

SUPPLIES
* 2 dozen 12-oz paper cups
* 3 cookie sheets or flat trays

Ancient Greek **architecture** often used a **post-and-lintel system**. You can see this in the Parthenon. In this system, posts (or columns) hold up a **horizontal** beam (a lintel). Post-and-lintel systems are very strong, as this experiment will demonstrate.

1 Turn a cup over and place it flat on the ground. What will happen if you stand on it? Make a prediction and then try it out.

2 Place more cups alongside each other and balance one of the trays on top of them. Stand on the cookie sheet. What happens?

3 Experiment to see how many cups you need underneath a cookie sheet to hold your weight.

4 Challenge yourself or a friend to see who can build the most layers of cups and cookie sheets that will hold your weight.

TRY THIS! How do you think using plastic cups (instead of paper cups) for this experiment would change the results? Give it a try and see what happens!

WORDS to KNOW

architecture: the style or look of a building.

post-and-lintel system: a building system where spaced, vertical posts hold up horizontal beams.

horizontal: straight across from side to side.

PROJECT!

GLOSSARY SCAVENGER HUNT

SUPPLIES
* pen or pencil
* this book

We've learned a lot of words in this book. Now it's time to have some fun with them!

1 Use the glossary to match these words to their definitions below.

- amphorae
- chiton
- ionic column
- Dionysus
- Olympics
- democracy
- grammatistes
- kylix
- Parthenon
- poleis
- debate
- frieze

Definitions:

- An ancient Greek teacher.
- A basic piece of clothing that men and women wore in ancient Greek times.
- To argue about something, to try to convince the other person of a point of view.
- Greek city-states.
- A grand and famous temple in Athens dedicated to the goddess Athena.
- The most popular sports contest in ancient Greece, now a global event held every four years.
- A form of government where people participate.
- A narrow horizontal, decorate panel.
- The god of wine.
- Pottery jars used to store wine and olive oil in ancient Greece.
- A shallow, two-handled cup used for drinking wine.
- A simple Greek column with a scroll-like top.

ANSWER ORDER: GRAMMATISTES, CHITON, DEBATE, POLEIS, PARTHENON, OLYMPICS, DEMOCRACY, FRIEZE, DIONYSUS, AMPHORAE, KYLIX, IONIC COLUMN.

PROJECT!

MODEL PARTHENON

The Parthenon was made of marble and wood. You can build your own model of the temple with some easy-to-find items.

SUPPLIES
* 8.5 x 11 white paper
* tape
* 2 shoebox lids, same size
* scissors
* marker
* white acrylic paint

1 Cut 14 pieces of the paper in half, width-wise. Roll each piece of paper around your marker to create a "column" that's 5½ inches tall. Use a piece of tape to keep your column from unraveling. Repeat the process until you have 28 columns. Depending on the size of the shoebox, you may need to adjust the number.

2 Turn over one of the lids so it looks like a serving tray. Tape your paper columns along the insides of the lid an equal distance from each other. There will be six columns along the short sides and eight columns along the long sides of the lid.

3 Place the other lid on top of the columns. The top of the lid should be facing up. Tape the columns to the inside of this top lid.

4 Paint your whole model with the white paint.

TRY THIS! After more than 2,000 years of damage, the Parthenon no longer has a complete roof. But you can make and add a V-shaped roof to your model using cardboard if you'd like.

PROJECT!

GREEK MYTH STORY

SUPPLIES
* paper
* pen, pencil, or markers

Ancient Greek myths and stories about gods have been popular since ancient times. Here's a chance to illustrate your own myth.

1 Read an ancient Greek myth. Some suggestions to get you started: King Midas and His Gold Touch, Achilles's Heel, Icarus and his Wings, Pandora's Box, Jason and the Argonauts, Perseus and Medusa, or Theseus and the Minotaur.

2 Decide on three to five key scenes that best tell the story. Think about the following. How does the story start? What happens in the middle? How does the story end?

3 Draw three to five boxes on your piece of paper, like a comic strip or a graphic novel. In the boxes, draw the key scenes of the myth. You can add text boxes or speech bubbles (the little cloud-like shapes that go over a character's head) to tell the story.

 **You can see a life-size movie prop of the famous Trojan Horse that now stands in Turkey.**

🔍 TROY HOUSE CANAKKALE

TRY THIS! Invite your friends or family members to illustrate their own Greek myth stories. Combine your story and their stories into a book.

GLOSSARY

abacus: an early calculator using beads on rods to add and subtract.

accessory: something, often jewelry, added to make an outfit more attractive.

acropolis: a fortified high area or hill where people went during a battle.

agora: the open marketplace in the middle of an ancient Greek town.

altar: a raised table for religious ceremonies.

amphorae: pottery jars used to store wine and olive oil.

ancient: from an early time in history.

andronitis: the men's area of an ancient Greek home.

andron: the area of a Greek home where the men entertained guests and held dinner parties.

antique: an object that's collectable or valuable because it is very old or historically important.

apprentice: someone who learns to do a job by working for someone who already does the job.

archaeologist: a scientist who studies ancient people and their cultures through the objects they left behind.

architecture: the style or look of a building.

artifact: an object made by people from past cultures, including tools, pottery, and jewelry.

Assembly: a group of 6,000 citizens in ancient Greece who met, discussed, and then voted on important matters in Athens.

astronomy: the study of the sun, moon, stars, planets, and space.

BCE: put after a date, BCE stands for Before Common Era and counts down to zero. CE stands for Common Era and counts up from zero. These non-religious terms correspond to BC and AD. This book was printed in 2019 CE.

brazier: a small stove used in an ancient Greek home.

brooch: a special pin.

bust: a sculpture of a person's head, shoulders, and chest.

cavalry: soldiers on horseback.

ceramic: made from clay.

chamber pot: a large, bowl-shaped pot used as an indoor toilet.

chiton: a basic piece of clothing that men and women wore in ancient Greek times.

chlamys: a short cloak worn by ancient Greeks.

citizen: a member of a city or country who enjoys certain rights.

city-state: an independent city that governs itself and the towns and land around it.

civilization: a community of people that is advanced in art, science, and government.

climate: the long-term weather patterns of a particular area of land.

column: a tall, thick post that holds up part of a building.

comedy: a funny play.

constellation: a group of stars in the sky that resembles a certain shape, such as the Big Dipper. There are 88 official constellations.

Corinthian column: a Greek column with an elaborate, leafy top.

83

GREEKS!

Council: a group of 500 ancient Greeks who made laws and chose military leaders.

courtyard: the small open-roofed area in the center of an ancient Greek home.

culture: the beliefs and way of life of a group of people.

debate: to argue about something, to try to convince the other person of a point of view.

democracy: a form of government where the people participate.

diameter: the line through the center of a circle, from one side to the other.

Dionysus: the god of wine.

Doric column: a Greek column with a plain top.

earthenware: pottery made of fired clay.

economics: having to do with the resources and wealth of a country.

epic: a long poem that tells of the deeds of a legendary hero.

exaggerate: to make something sound larger, greater, better, or worse than it really is.

exedra: a covered porch in ancient Greek homes.

ferment: when a substance breaks down over time into another substance, such as grape juice turning into wine.

foundation: the base of a home that is partly underground and supports the weight of the building.

frieze: a narrow, horizontal, decorative panel.

garos: a sauce made from old fish, used in ancient Greece.

geometric: straight lines and simple shapes such as circles or squares.

goddess: a female god.

grammatistes: an ancient Greek teacher.

greaves: a piece of armor used to protect the shin.

gynaeconitis: the women's area of an ancient Greek home.

Hellas: the term used by ancient Greeks to describe their region.

Hellenes: the term used by ancient Greeks to describe themselves.

Heraia: an Olympic-style competition for women.

himation: a large piece of material that the ancient Greeks wore over their shoulders.

Homer: a famous ancient Greek poet who created the *Iliad* and the *Odyssey*.

hoplite: a Greek foot soldier.

horizontal: straight across from side to side.

Ionic column: a simple Greek column with a scroll-like top.

juror: someone who is part of a jury.

jury: a group of people who hear a case in court. Jurors give their opinion, called a verdict.

kitharistes: a teacher who taught music in ancient Greece.

kline: a long couch on which guests lay at ancient Greek dinner parties.

knucklebones: a game where players tossed small bones into the air and tried to catch them.

kylix: a shallow, two-handled cup used for drinking wine.

GLOSSARY

laurel: a wreath made of olive leaves that Olympic winners wore on their heads.

Long Walls: long stone walls that protected the road between Athens and its port of Piraeus.

lyre: a musical instrument similar to a small harp.

malleable: able to be hammered, pressed, or shaped without breaking.

mathematics: the study of ideas related to numbers. Mathematicians study mathematics.

melting point: the temperature at which a solid becomes a liquid.

military: the armed forces of a country.

mosaic: a picture or design made from tiny tiles or stones set in cement.

Mount Olympus: the mountain where the ancient Greek gods lived.

mudbrick: a brick made using clay, pebbles, straw, and water and dried in the sun.

myth: a traditional story dealing with ancestors or heroes or even supernatural figures.

narrator: someone who tells or helps tell a story.

oikos: an ancient Greek household, including family members and slaves.

Olympics: the most popular sports contest in ancient Greece, now a global event held every four years.

oracle: a woman in ancient Greece who supposedly spoke for the gods and offered advice.

orchestra: an area in front of the stage where the chorus performed in ancient Greek plays.

pankration: a brutal sport of the ancient Greek Olympics that combined boxing and wrestling.

papyrus: paper made from the papyrus plant.

parallel: two lines always the same distance apart.

Parthenon: a grand and famous temple in Athens dedicated to the goddess Athena.

pentathlon: an Olympic event that includes five sports. In ancient times, the contests included discus and javelin throwing, running, long jumping, and wrestling.

Persian Empire: an ancient empire to the south and east of Greece.

petasos: a flat, wide-brimmed hat that ancient Greeks wore.

philosopher: a person who studies knowledge, truth, and the nature of reality.

philosophy: the study of truth, wisdom, the nature of reality, and knowledge.

plague: a serious disease that spreads quickly to many people and often causes death.

plains: large, flat land areas.

polis: a Greek city-state.

post-and-lintel system: a building system where spaced, vertical posts hold up horizontal beams.

satire: plays that poke fun at leaders or serious issues.

scrolls: pieces of papyrus glued together and rolled up.

slave: a person who, in the eyes of the law, belongs to another person.

solidify: to become hard or solid.

sphere: round, like a ball.

GREEKS!

suburb: an area at the outer edges of a city, usually made up of homes with few businesses.

surrender: to admit defeat and give up.

symposium: a party where Greek men gathered to eat, drink, and discuss topics.

temple: a building in which people worship gods and practice their religion.

tendon: tissue that connects muscles to bones.

terra-cotta: earthen clay used as a building material, for pottery, and for sculptures.

thalamos: the master bedroom of an ancient Greek home.

thronos: a highly ornate, high-backed chair used in ancient Greece.

tiers: rows arranged one above another.

torso: the human body except the head, arms, and legs.

trade: the buying, selling, or exchange of goods and services.

tragedy: a sad play.

tutor: a private teacher.

uncivilized: crude, not very advanced.

underworld: in Greek mythology, the place beneath the earth where people believed the souls of the dead went.

vegetarian: someone who doesn't eat meat.

veil: a thin covering that goes over a person's head.

vertical: straight up and down.

votive: something that is a symbol for a wish.

METRIC CONVERSIONS

Use this chart to find the metric equivalents to the English measurements in this book. If you need to know a half measurement, divide by two. If you need to know twice the measurement, multiply by two. How do you find a quarter measurement? How do you find three times the measurement?

English	Metric
1 inch	2.5 centimeters
1 foot	30.5 centimeters
1 yard	0.9 meter
1 mile	1.6 kilometers
1 pound	0.5 kilogram
1 teaspoon	5 milliliters
1 tablespoon	15 milliliters
1 cup	237 milliliters

RESOURCES

BOOKS

Bordessa, Kris. *Tools of Ancient Greeks*. Nomad Press, 2006.

MacDonald, Fiona. *I Wonder Why Greeks Built Temples: and Other Questions about Ancient Greece*. Kingfisher, 2012.

Napoli, Donna Jo. *Treasury of Greek Mythology: Classic Stories of Gods, Goddesses, Heroes and Monsters*. National Geographic Children's Books, 2011.

Pearson, Anne. *DK Eyewitness Books: Ancient Greece*. DK Children, 2014.

WEBSITES

Ancient Greece for Kids: youtube.com/watch?v=wgvlzcPqPLU

DKFindOut: Ancient Greece: dkfindout.com/us/search/ancient-greece

Explore Ancient Greece: childrensuniversity.manchester.ac.uk/learning-activities/history/ancient-greece/explore-ancient-greece

Guide to Ancient Greece: historyforkids.net/ancient-greece.html

National Geographic Kids: 10 Facts About Ancient Greece: natgeokids.com/za/discover/history/greece/10-facts-about-the-ancient-greeks

MUSEUMS

The Cleveland Museum of Art (Cleveland, Ohio): clevelandart.org

The Metropolitan Museum of Art (New York, New York): metmuseum.org

Los Angeles County Museum of Art (Los Angeles, California): lacma.org

The Detroit Institute of Arts (Detroit, Michigan): dia.org

Museum of Fine Arts (Boston, Massachusetts): mfa.org

Nelson-Atkins Museum of Art (Kansas City, Missouri): nelson-atkins.org

University of Pennsylvania Museum (Philadelphia, Pennsylvania): penn.museum

GREEKS!

ESSENTIAL QUESTIONS

Introduction: How was ancient Greece similar to today's world?

Chapter 1: How were ancient Greek houses different on the outside and the inside?

Chapter 2: What crops were important to ancient Greeks?

Chapter 3: How does the climate affect what you wear?

Chapter 4: What subjects were important to ancient Greek students?

Chapter 5: How are the modern Olympics different from the ancient Olympics?

Chapter 6: How is ancient Greek democracy different from today's democracy?

Chapter 7: How did religion play a part in the lives of ancient Greeks?

QR CODE GLOSSARY

Page v: merriam-webster.com

Page 13: sciencealert.com/three-stunning-ancient-greek-mosaics-unearthed-on-the-syrian-border

Page 25: thorvaldsensmuseum.dk/en/collections/work/H526

Page 35: metmuseum.org/toah/hd/grdr/hd_grdr.htm

Page 43: youtube.com/watch?v=8EECNgK_Cv0

Page 55: youtube.com/watch?v=jjt-c282q3A

Page 66: youtube.com/watch?v=B9dhvsW8oFI

Page 75: americanart.si.edu/artwork/trojan-horse-17255

Page 82: canakkaleotelleri.com/en/places-to-visit/city-center/troy-horse-statue

INDEX

A
Achilles, 73
acropolis, 4, 5, 10, 77
activities (Projects)
 Black-Figure Vase, 31
 Defend Yourself!, 69
 Glossary Scavenger Hunt, 80
 Greek Myth Story, 82
 Host a Symposium, 30
 Jury Tokens, 67
 Knucklebones, 50
 Long-Jump Contest, 59
 Make a Brooch, 38
 Make a Chiton, 37
 Make a Courtyard Column, 18–19
 Make a Field Notebook, 8–9
 Make a Kylix, 26–27
 Make a Laurel Wreath, 58
 Make a Model of an Oil Lamp, 17
 Make a Mosaic, 20
 Make a Water Clock, 68
 Make Olive Oil Soap, 28–29
 Model Parthenon, 81
 Olive Oil Foot Scrub, 39
 Play "Storm the Acropolis," 10
 Poetry Scroll, 47
 Post-and-Lintel Experiment, 79
 Pump It Up!, 48–49
 Theater Mask, 60–61
Alexander the Great, v, 66
alphabet, Greek, 44
Aphrodite, 72, 74
Apollo, 72, 75
Archimedes/Archimedes' screw, 42–43, 48–49
Ares, 72
Aristotle, 45–46
art, 14, 35, 42, 61, 75, 76. See also mosaics; music; poetry; pottery/vases
Artemis, 72
Athena, 51, 72, 77
Athens, iv–v, 4–6, 45, 51, 55, 62–65, 77
athletics and physical fitness, iv, 6, 41, 51–55, 58–59

B
bathing, 13, 23, 39
buildings. See homes; temples

C
chitons, 33–34, 37
city-states, iv, 4–6, 10, 51–53, 62, 65, 78. See also Athens
climate/weather, 3, 12, 32, 34, 53
clothes and shoes, 15, 32–39, 53
coins, iv, 78
columns, 18–19, 76–77, 79
Coubertin, Pierre de, 55

D
Demeter, 72
democracy, iv, 5, 62–64
Dionysus, 14, 24, 72–73

E
education, 40–47. See also mathematics; philosophy; science
entertainment, iv–v, 13, 22, 30, 46, 50, 51–61, 71

F
farming, 3, 22–25
food and drink, 21–30. See also farming
furniture, 15–16, 22

G
games, 46, 50. See also entertainment
geography, 2–3. See also climate/weather
gods and goddesses, 12, 14, 23, 24, 45, 51–53, 55, 57, 70–78
golden ratio, 61
Greece, Ancient
 city-states in. See Athens; city-states
 clothes and shoes in, 15, 32–39, 53
 democracy in, iv, 5, 62–64
 education in, 40–47. See also mathematics; philosophy; science
 entertainment in, iv–v, 13, 22, 30, 46, 50, 51–61, 71
 food in. See farming; food and drink
 geography and map of, 2–3. See also climate/weather

homes in, 11–20
legacies of, 1, 42–43, 54–55, 62, 78
military and war in. *See* military; war and defense
religion in. *See* gods and goddesses; temples
Romans and, v, 3, 6, 55
studying of, 1–2, 7
timeline of, iv–v

H

Hades, 72
hairstyles, 35
Hellenes/Hellas, 3
Hephaestus, 23, 72
Hera, 53, 72
Hermes, 12, 72
Hippocrates, 42–43
Homer, *Iliad* and *Odyssey*, iv, 49, 74
homes, 11–20
hoplites, 65–66, 69

I

Iliad (Homer), iv, 49, 74

J

jewelry, 34, 36, 38
juries and trials, 64, 67–68

L

Long Walls, v, 6

M

map, 2
mathematics, iv, 40–44, 61
Mead, Roderick, 75
men/boys, 5–6, 13, 14–15, 33–37, 41, 52–53, 57, 63
Midas, King, 72–73
military, 5–6, 41, 51, 65–66, 69. *See also* war and defense
mosaics, 13, 20
music, 22, 42
myths, 57, 72–75, 82

O

Odyssey (Homer), iv, 49
oikos, 15
olive oil, 17, 23, 28–29, 39, 53
Olympics, iv, 52–55, 58–59

P

Panathenaic Games, 51
Parthenon, v, 4, 76, 77, 78, 79, 81
Phidias, 61
philosophy, 22, 43–46
Plato, 45
poetry, iv, 22, 41, 47, 49, 74
Poseidon, 72
pottery/vases, 9, 16, 24, 25, 26–27, 31, 35, 42
Pythagoras, iv, 42–43

R

religion. *See* gods and goddesses; temples
Romans, v, 3, 6, 55

S

Schliemann, Heinrich, 74
science, iv, 7, 42–44, 46
Socrates, v, 44–45
Sparta, 5

T

temples, v, 4, 23, 76–79, 81
theater, v, 56–57, 60–61
timeline, iv–v
Trojan War/Trojan Horse, 73–75, 78, 82

V

vases/pottery, 9, 16, 24, 25, 26–27, 31, 35, 42

W

war and defense, v, 4, 6, 10, 53, 65–66, 69, 73–75. *See also* military
weather/climate, 3, 12, 32, 34, 53
women/girls, 6, 14–15, 22, 33–37, 40, 46, 52–53, 57, 71

Z

Zeus, 52, 71, 72, 74